Beating Prostate Cancer
Hormonal Therapy & Diet

Beating Prostate Cancer
Hormonal Therapy & Diet

by Dr. Charles "Snuffy" Myers

Rivanna Health Publications, LLC
Charlottesville, Virginia

Copyright © 2006 Rivanna Health Publications, LLC
All rights reserved.
First Edition, 2006.
Printed in the United States of America.

09 08 07 06 05 04 03   5 4 3 2 1

Library of Congress Cataloging-in-Publication Data.

CONTENTS

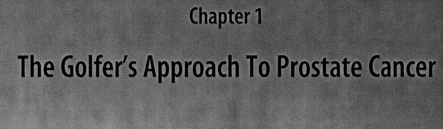

Chapter 1

The Golfer's Approach To Prostate Cancer

While there are over 4,000 research papers published every year and a great number of books that present an overview of the various "conventional" treatment options, there is, to date, no *comprehensive* patient resource on hormonal therapy—also called androgen blockade—a sad fact because it's quickly becoming a major point of interest for men with prostate cancer.

While many men will face the "conventional" treatments for prostate cancer, whether it's radiation, surgery, or chemotherapy, it is quite likely that they will also undergo hormonal therapy in conjunction with these treatments or if these treatments fail. The parameters for failure or recurrence for these treatments vary depending on the patient, but it's important to note that hormonal therapy can stall or even prevent recurrence for many men. In fact, as I will mention later, there are even some cases where hormonal therapy alone has been very successful in pushing prostate cancer into remission.

Why Golf?

A successful golfer combines intelligence, strength, resilience, strategy, patience, and skill and uses these elements in various patterns to find the most efficient route to the green. While other sports use brute force, speed, or a well-honed talent to achieve their desired results, none of these traits alone would be very effective in approaching a prostate cancer diagnosis. The truth is that you'll need to develop all of these traits as you fight your way toward remission.

This is why the golf metaphor is so useful for prostate cancer treatment. Just as a golf game is based on unique variables—some controlled and other extraneous, each persons' cancer is likewise unique and needs to be treated as such. Since prostate cancer is a variable disease with levels of aggressiveness that go from mild health concerns to life threatening issues, it makes sense that each man's treatment be equally varied. Depending on the type of cancer you have, the time it is diagnosed, and its stage at the time of diagnosis, we have to develop a strategy based on the reality of your case or, in other words, we have to play it as it lies.

While it would be optimal for physicians to shoot a hole-in-one with their treatment, or effect a curative outcome in one try, this is not always realistic. Often we need to overcome many obstacles, gracefully maneuvering through all of those twists and turns along the way.

And sometimes it is quite possible to get on the green under par—or create a treatment strategy that adds years to your life—after what appear to be major setbacks early on. In other words, I've seen many men beat odds that seem insurmountable, utilizing a combination of treatments of which hormonal therapy was an integral part, men who are still cancer-free today.

As a physician specializing in prostate cancer treatment, the most important thing I've learned is that carefully planning your way out of the sand trap and onto the green is greatly hinged on an intimate relationship with all of the tools in your proverbial golf bag as well as a detailed understanding of the terrain of the course. As a patient living with prostate cancer, I learned that by educating myself first and then formulating a well-crafted strategy that made maximal benefit of these tools, I was able to force what would be considered a remission while preserving my overall health and longevity.

In the following pages, I'll present my recommendations on hormonal therapy as both a medical oncologist and a patient, including a Patient Profile section so both patients and physicians can have a written account of how effective this treatment can be for men at almost every cancer stage.

My goal in presenting this or any other material is to provide men and their families with education and, thus, hope, in a simple format they can use today. This industry as a whole often pushes men into treatment without considering the course—or the consequences—and physicians sometimes hide behind the technical terms inherent to scientific language, which only further confuses the patient at a time when making clear decisions is crucial to their survival.

We designed this book to be a straightforward, hands-on guide that you can take to your doctor to aid in discussions about your treatment options. After all, prostate cancer treatment is a dialogue between you, your medical team, and the ever-growing body of available literature. This book is meant to be an interactive tool for facilitating that dialogue, with large margins for note taking and sections that appeal to veteran readers of the *Prostate Forum* as well as the newly diagnosed. We have culled together the best of what we've done on this issue in our *Prostate Forum* and *Living Longer* newsletters, and added new material, including new case studies, and an advanced section on vitamins and supplements. At best, the book will be a road map to help you find the right treatment; at worst it will be another useful tool in your prostate-cancer golf bag. The good news is the more tools you have available to you, the more likely you are to be prepared for all of the struggles that lay ahead, and this, I think, is something to feel optimistic about.

Be optomistic

When I was first diagnosed I had a very aggressive case of cancer that involved metastatic spread to my lymph nodes. I discussed my case with quite a few of my colleagues. In general, the assessment was that I almost certainly would be ill with advanced disease by five years and would likely die within ten. While I do take some satisfaction that my PSA is now undetectable more than seven years after the diagnosis, my course wasn't easy. But the single most important thing I did was to take the attitude that I would do whatever I could to gain control over my cancer. Even if I ended up dying of prostate cancer, I wanted to know that I had done everything possible to avoid that end. I chose a very aggressive form of treatment that involved surgically removing the lymph nodes in the back of my abdomen. I followed this procedure with external beam radiation and brachytherapy to attack the remaining cancer in my prostate and then underwent eighteen months of aggressive hormonal therapy to deprive the remaining cells of the androgens on which they thrive. I also adopted a Mediterranean heart-healthy diet and began to take a short list of supplements that, according to current research, limit the spread of prostate cancer or reduce the risk of dying from it.

I realize that as a prostate cancer specialist I had a leg up on the typical patient, which is why I like to stress how important and empowering it is to educate yourself in a time when it's easy to despair.

Too often pessimism and, ultimately, depression can affect the way men view their disease, their treatment, and the success of their chosen program. In fact, over the years I've found myself asking if pessimism is as deadly a disease as prostate cancer itself.

This question can be answered in many ways, I think. I suppose creating some disease criteria would be helpful in answering this question. Is a disease something that affects our daily life? Is it something that at times can be so overwhelming it pervades every action until it dominates even the way we think about ourselves? Does it affect our loved ones in the process? Will it reduce years from our lives? If one uses these criteria to describe a disease then, yes, pessimism certainly qualifies. We all know people, call them cynics, realists, etc. and so on, who are constantly focused on the negative. To them the world is a cruel and heartless place where nothing good ever happens—or where everything good in this world simply doesn't happen to them.

Think about how much time they spend dwelling on these issues, how much energy they expend on them, and how much energy it takes just to listen to their litany of complaints about this world. Whether they feel entitled or depressed, that everything is their fault or that nothing is, this kind of thinking all leads people to the same place: desperation and despair.

I do find it interesting that this idea is firmly fixed in our culture. How often have we heard that John Doe just died because "he gave up"? In contrast, the cliché "where there is a will, there is a way" also comes to mind. I deal with life and death issues everyday and time and again I have seen people give up and die long before they should have. In contrast, I have patients whose disease is so aggressive that their other doctors urge them to put their affairs in order and yet they refuse to give up. These kind of relentless optimists continually seek out new and better treatments and beat all odds. In the book *Survivor Stories*, edited by my daughter and son-in-law, you'll find several such stories—in fact one woman received a call from a medical institution some years after she received her "death sentence" from them.

"We've noticed that you're still alive," they said. "Do you mind coming in for a few tests?"

While this is purely anecdotal evidence, the medical community sees anomalies like this all the time. Is it simply optimism that keeps these people alive or is it pessimism that kills? Folk wisdom suggests that pessimism is the mistake and now it seems that the medical literature also supports this idea.

The article that triggered my thoughts on this subject appeared in the *Archives of General Psychiatry* in 2004 (Giltay, et al 61:1126-1135). In this Dutch study, 466 men and 475 women between the ages of 65 and 85 took a test to determine their relative optimism versus pessimism. They were then followed from 1991 to 2001. During that time, there were 397 deaths. The optimists had a death rate close to half that of the pessimists. The deaths from cardiovascular disease, largely heart attack and stroke, were down by 77% in the optimist group compared with the pessimists. There was a similar study in the journal *Psychosomatic Medicine* last year that showed a marked worsening in carotid atherosclerosis in pessimists compared with optimists (Mathews, et al 66:640-644). Finally, the Mayo Clinic reported similar results that involved following optimists versus pessimists for greater than 30 years (Mayo Clinic Proceedings 77: 748-753).

How is it that optimists do better than pessimists? It appears that these two approaches to life have a very different impact on human biology. In one recent article, Steptoe, et al. measured cortisol, the major stress hormone in the body, and found that levels were lowest in those who rated themselves as happy (Steptoe, et al. Proceedings of the National Academy of Science USA 102: 6508, 2005). One key event in the evolution of heart disease is the appearance of blood clots in the major arteries. Steptoe, et al. found elevated fibrinogen levels, a major risk factor for heart disease, in those who rated themselves as unhappy.

My own observations suggest that the picture is far worse than these articles indicate. Not only do pessimists do worse medically, but also they're absolutely miserable while they wait for bad things to happen. For the optimist, time is usually passed pleasantly because he or she anticipates that whatever bad things might happen, tomorrow will most likely be good. I am reminded of my great uncle who died at age 98. He had experienced a wide range of medical illnesses and was never able to qualify for life insurance. When he was in his 80s, I asked him the reason for his long life. He said that you can always expect to get sick. The secret was figuring out a way to get well. This is how he approached each of his many illnesses: he assumed there was a way to get well again. He managed to practice dentistry from his mid 20s until his retirement at age 93. Every day for more than 70 years, he walked one mile from his home to his office and then back home each evening. During that time, he dealt with thyroid and prostate cancer, heart attack, pacemaker implantation, hypertension and a severe case of giardiasis. After each challenge, he would marshal his resources and bounce back. He only stopped practicing denistry when his visual acuity declined to the point where he could no longer perform.

Sometimes pessimism is just a manifestation of an underlying depression. If this is the case, I think these papers strongly support actively treating depression. This may involve drugs. For example, I have had considerable success with both Welbutrin and Lexapro as treatment for the depression that commonly develops when men are on hormonal therapy. You also need to be aware that exercise can markedly lessen depression in many people. In this very book, we discuss vitamin D and sunlight exposure which greatly influence the positive impact of a well-planned hormonal therapy regimen. It has long been known that exposure to sunlight can lessen depression in many people. Now it appears that a good deal of that is due to vitamin D.

Nevertheless, a portion of pessimism is not founded in depression but in an approach to life, which is based on diminished expectations. And it's hard not to let disappointments get you down when you see others thriving around you. The truth is that life is full of disappointments for all of us, but by focusing on this, aren't you creating a self-fulfilling prophecy in which your only consolation is that you happened to be right in the middle of a catastrophe? Remember: the pessimist has his worst fears confirmed and unexpectedly good things happen to optimists!

As a hormonal therapy patient with an undetectable PSA, I'm living proof of that.

Chapter 2
What Is Complete Remission?

Now that we have you in a positive frame of mind and you're ready to go out and beat your cancer, we need to explore the concept of a complete remission.

We can now cure a number of cancers even if they are metastatic. This is true for acute lymphocytic leukemia in children, Hodgkins disease, nonHodgkins lymphoma, and testicular cancer. In each of these diseases, cure is most likely if the patient rapidly enters a complete remission, typically within 4 months of starting treatment. If we can't create a complete remission, cure simply isn't possible. For each of these cancers I just mentioned, complete remission means that we can find no evidence of cancer after treatment. Among individuals who attain a complete remission, some have microscopic deposits of cancer that will re-grow over time. Thus, the ultimate measure of successful treatment is for the person to remain in complete remission for years after treatment is over. This is called a durable, un-maintained complete remission. As you'll see, it's possible to attain complete remission in men with metastatic prostate cancer, **but these remissions are not durable if they aren't maintained.**

Nevertheless, my approach to men with metastatic disease is governed by the knowledge that it's now possible to place many into complete remission. Based on what we know about treating cancers with drugs, this approach is likely to give any man the best chance of long-term survival.

So: complete remission in men with metastatic prostate cancer means that no evidence of the cancer can be found. By this I mean that the PSA is less than 0.05 ng/ml.

Furthermore, bone scan and CT scan results show no evidence of remaining cancer. My current views on this subject were formed following a provocative discussion with David Crawford, the head of Urology at University of Colorado. In 1989, he published a major randomized controlled trial comparing Lupron alone with Lupron + Eulexin. In this trial, Crawford and his colleagues noted that a certain proportion of men with advanced metastatic disease entered complete remission on hormonal therapy. In this influential discussion, he expounded upon this by noting that many of these men remained disease-free for many years. It is important to note that the men in the trial were on continuous hormonal therapy, so these are maintained complete remissions.

Now, at my clinic I commonly use intermittent hormonal therapy. The thing that has surprised me most about this approach is that there are a proportion of men who remain in complete remission for years after treatment ends. Dr. Robert Leibowitz of Compassionate Oncology reports that this is common if we administer Proscar during the time patients are off hormonal therapy. My own experience with intermittent hormonal therapy supports the contention that drugs that prevent the synthesis of dihydrotestosterone (DHT), like Proscar or Avodart, do what Dr. Leibowitz claims. One of the first patients I treated in this fashion started hormonal therapy in April 1996 and stopped in April 1997. Since then, we've used Proscar to maintain his disease; his PSA has remained undetectable for more than 8 years despite having a normal testosterone for more than 6 years. Thus, while it is possible to attain a complete remission in metastatic prostate cancer, these remissions are not durable if they are not maintained.

Based on these experiences, I divide prostate cancer treatment into two phases. The first phase focuses on attaining a complete remission. The second phase is designed to delay or prevent disease recurrence. In large, all of my efforts are focused on either obtaining as complete a response as possible or in looking for better agents to maintain a remission.

My current program for newly diagnosed men with metastatic cancer is to first try to induce a complete remission with triple hormonal blockade using LHRH agonists, such as Lupron, Trelstar, Eligard or Zoladex, combined with Casodex and either Proscar or Avodart. If the patient does not enter a complete remission with this program, I use second line hormonal therapy with agents such as ketoconazole, transdermal estrogen, or aminoglutethimide.

Taxotere-based chemotherapy is only initiated after second line hormonal therapy is no longer causing the PSA to decline. The advantage of this approach is that many of my patients don't receive chemotherapy and thus are spared the often severe side effects of this form of treatment. On the other hand, if you do need chemotherapy, you can start treatment at a time when the amount of cancer present has been reduced to a minimum. These are conditions where chemotherapy is likely to be most effective.

Tools For Complete Remission

I think it is important for you to know that my thinking about this subject started with my own disease. When I was diagnosed, my first PSA was over 20. I was 55 years old. I had a Gleason 7 cancer on the left side and it had spread to my seminal vesicle on that side and then leaked from the seminal vesicle to the lymph nodes in my pelvis. There were cancer cells in my blood stream and bone marrow on both sides of my pelvis. While it apparently hadn't started to grow (because the bone scan was negative), the cancer cells had clearly gotten outside the gland and had spread everywhere. As I said in the introduction, the consensus of my professional colleagues was that I would be sick with advanced metastatic disease in five years and dead by the tenth.

So in my own case, how did I address this grievous situation and how did my experience alter how I approach treatment? Just as with golf, I had to play the ball from where it lay. I decided that I would find each place occupied by cancer and then ask myself which tool (or golf club) would be best to address the cancer at that site. Part of deciding whether you need a 9-iron or a sand wedge is to honestly and accurately evaluate where the ball is and how to play around the obstacles in its path.

And for prostate cancer that means accurate staging. My ProstaScint scan showed cancer in my pelvic lymph nodes and in one node in the back of my abdomen about the level of my kidney. While the pelvic nodes could be treated with radiation therapy, the one in the back of my abdomen could not. I went to Johns Hopkins University where they used laparscopy to strip all the lymph nodes from the renal arteries down to the point where the lymph node chain left the abdominal cavity. This was my best bet to take care of the lymph node in the back of my abdomen.

I then started on hormonal therapy with Lupron, Casodex, and Proscar—the triple hormonal blockade that I have since come to use in most of my patients. By May, my PSA was undetectable. I then traveled to see Dr. Dattoli, then at Community Memorial Hostpital in Tampa, Florida, for very aggressive radiation therapy and seed implantation. I also continued on hormonal therapy for 18 months. If I were diagnosed today I would only take hormonal therapy for 12 months, but back then I didn't know what I know now. In 1999, the standard was three years of Lupron as a single agent and I didn't fully appreciate how much better triple hormonal blockade actually is. On the 18th month, I decided I'd had enough. I can only say that doctors who recommend continuous hormonal therapy haven't tried it! So, in August of 2000, I stopped Lupron and Casodex but continued on Proscar as the key element of my maintenance program.

By that point I'd become convinced that a heart-healthy diet was one of the things that you could do during maintenance to keep the cancer from coming back. This conviction was based on research that I did when I was at the University of Virginia on arachidonic acid, the fat found in red meat, dairy fat, and egg yolks. Today there are more than 100 papers in the scientific literature on how arachidonic acid can promote the growth and spread of prostate cancer. So diet became a critical part of my maintenance program. At the end of hormonal therapy, I weighed 209 pounds. (And I'm only 5'8"!) After several years on this diet, as well as a carefully designed exercise program, I now weigh 145 pounds, which is more appropriate for my height and frame. The diet I used is outlined later in this book, and, in more detail in our nutrition guide, *Eating Your Way to Better Health.*

It has now been a little more than seven years since my diagnosis. In the process of working through my own treatment, I created a treatment system that involves causing a complete remission and then maintaining it. It was in this process that I developed the strategy outlined in this book. To explore the golfing metaphor further, my own experience led to the clubs I now have in my bag and how I use them depends as much on the big picture as it does on the terrain of any specific hole.

Chapter 3
Where The Ball Lands

Staging is the process of determining how far the cancer has spread. Most cancers are staged using what is called the TNM approach. T stands for tumor and includes information on the size of the original cancer within the prostate gland and whether it has spread from one side of the gland to the opposite side. We also determine if the tumor has spread outside the gland to adjacent organs. N stands for lymph nodes and includes information on the number of lymph nodes involved and where they are located. M stands for metastases and includes information on whether the cancer has spread to bone, lung, liver, or other sites.

Staging is crucial because it plays a central role in deciding which form of treatment is best. If you want a plan that might offer ten, twenty, or thirty years of disease control, you want a treatment plan that will kill all of the cancer wherever it has spread.

The first step is to determine the extent of cancer within the actual prostate gland. It has long been clear that the standard transrectal ultrasound and biopsy underestimate the extent of prostate cancer within the gland. Furthermore, this approach misses small but aggressive cancers in more than 20% of cases. There are three techniques that can improve these results. The endorectal MRI can provide a more detailed view of the contents of the gland and some studies suggest it can be particularly useful in detecting cancer penetration of the prostatic capsule. Color Doppler ultrasound sees areas of increased blood flow—a characteristic of aggressive cancers capable of rapid growth and spread. The final technique is called saturation biopsy. Routine prostate biopsy protocols call for six to eighteen individual biopsies of the prostate gland. However, as stated above, this approach often misses the true extent of the cancer and can miss small areas of very aggressive cancer. Saturation biopsy gets around this problem by brute force and involves taking 40-70 biopsies using a grid to ensure full coverage in each part of the gland. While this requires anesthesia, and therefore a hospital admission, it seems, in general, to be surprisingly well tolerated. I have seen enough cases to say that saturation biopsy is the most complete of the three. For those unwilling to undergo such an aggressive biopsy procedure, the color Doppler has been consistently more useful than endorectal MRI. The biggest problem of the latter is that the tool has difficulty distinguishing cancer from previous biopsy bleeding.

The next step in staging is to evaluate lymph node involvement. CAT and MRI scans are widely used for this purpose, but are completely inadequate. Studies consistently show that these techniques only identify 15-30% of known lymph node metastases. The ProstaScint scan, especially when fused with the CAT scan, is far superior and can detect 80% of known areas of lymph node involvement. While not perfect, ProstaScint + CAT scan is the current state of the art diagnostic tool. A new technique, the Combidex scan, uses iron nanoparticles and claims to be able to detect cancers less than 1 mm across in lymph nodes. Unfortunately, this technique is still investigational; its true value remains uncertain.

The bone scan has long been the standard means for detecting bone metastases. However, any trauma to bone will also cause a positive bone scan. The MRI is very useful in differentiating trauma from bone involvement with cancer and should be used if the bone scan is at all ambiguous. When prostate cancer invades bone, it can cause new bone formation. This happens because prostate cancer activates the osteoblast, the key cell involved in bone formation. The osteoblast releases a protein, called bone-specific alkaline phosphatase, and the serum level of this protein increases as prostate cancer invades bone.

Cancer spread to other tissues, such as lung or liver, is relatively uncommon and is best detected by the CAT scan.

How Does Prostate Cancer Spread?

Before we move on to hormonal therapy, we need to talk a little more about where and how prostate cancer spreads throughout the body.

Spreading Into The Blood Stream

The prostate gland has a rich blood supply. Prostate cancer can leave the gland by moving through the wall of the prostate blood vessels into the venous blood. We normally think of the veins as simple pipes taking used blood from tissues throughout the body back to the heart and lungs. But in the pelvis, and extending back toward the spinal column, the veins form a complex network in which blood flows back and forth. If the prostate cancer cells enter this network, they can travel directly back to the spine and establish themselves there. This is why the most common site for bone metastases is in the lumbar and sacral spine. The cancer cells in the blood can also ascend to the right side of the heart, where they are then pumped into the lungs. The cancer cells can lodge in the lung wall, but only rarely grow large enough to detect and even then generally don't impair lung function. The cells that pass through the lungs are then pumped out to the rest of the body by the left side of the heart. While this path can lead the cancer cells anywhere in the body, they can actually only grow in the liver, which is rare, or in the adrenal gland and bone, which are common. They can also pass through tissues and enter the venous blood once again.

In my case, we found cancer cells in venous blood drawn from my forearm. In order to get there, they would have passed through the heart and lungs and been pumped out to the muscles and skin of the forearm before appearing in the venous blood of the forearm. The very fact that prostate cancer cells can commonly be detected in forearm venous blood (which cannot be coming from the venous blood draining the prostate gland) indicates just how widespread the cancer cells often are at the time of diagnosis.

Spreading Into The Lymph Nodes

Before you can understand the importance of cancer spread to the lymph nodes, you need to first understand the function of the lymphatic system. As the arteries enter tissues, they subdivide into progressively smaller branches. In the smallest vessels, called capillaries, oxygen and food are released into the tissues and carbon dioxide and other wastes removed. To facilitate the transfer of these and other blood components, the capillaries are leaky. A wide variety of proteins and fluid constantly exit the capillaries and enter the tissues. Without such an escape path, this fluid would accumulate in the tissues, causing edema.

Fortunately, the lymphatic vessels are open-ended tubes that can drain this fluid out of the tissues and channel it back toward the heart. All of the lymph nodes from the lower extremities and pelvis merge into one large pipe in the back of the abdomen. This large pipe passes up through the middle of the chest, gathering fluid from the lungs and exiting into the venous blood behind the clavicle on the left.

If this were the complete story, any parasite or bacteria that entered your tissues through a wound would rapidly gain access to your blood, which has potentially devastating consequences. To avoid just such a scenario, the body has established a rather sophisticated defense system. First, various white blood cells involved in killing invaders also constantly exit the capillaries and enter the tissues of the body, thereby placing them in position to handle bacteria and parasites. These same white cells enter the lymph channels and could travel upward with any invading bacteria, virus or parasite. And the lymphatic channels pass through four to five lymph nodes on their way to the blood stream. Each lymph node acts like a filtering device, capturing invading organisms. Once trapped in the node, an elaborate process takes place that aims to kill the invading organism. I am sure you have seen this in action. If you get an infection in your throat, the lymph nodes in your neck enlarge as they fight the infection. Likewise, if you have a boil on your legs, the nodes in your groin enlarge and become tender.

All tissues have lymphatic drainage, including the prostate gland. This means that the prostate cancer cells can enter the lymphatic system from the prostate gland. The cancer cells that escape the prostate gland to invade surrounding fatty tissues or the seminal vesicles can then enter the lymphatic channels that drain these sites. The lymphatic channels serving the prostate gland and surrounding tissues pass through the lymph nodes along the major arteries in the pelvis, especially those along the internal and external iliac artery. The cancer cells can proceed directly to these nodes along the arteries, or they can follow a more circuitous route. Sometimes the cells enter the lymph nodes immediately adjacent to the prostate gland or they pass through to lymph nodes at the back of the pelvis next to the sacrum. The lymph nodes in these two areas are those most commonly involved with prostate cancer. For reasons that are not entirely clear, it's more likely for prostate cancer cells to infiltrate the iliac nodes on the left side of the body, even if the cancer is on the right side of the prostate. If you're at high risk for lymph node spread because of a high Gleason grade, high PSA, or tumor size, many surgeons will biopsy your pelvic nodes before doing a radical prostatectomy. But they never sample nodes next to the sacrum because those are difficult to reach.

Once in the pelvic lymph nodes, the natural path of cancer spread is up the lymphatic chain into the abdomen, chest, and then on to the venous blood behind the left clavicle. There is a node right next to the point where lymphatic channel empties into the veins behind the left clavicle. This lymph node is called Virchow's node, named after one of the major German pathologists of the 1800's, Rudolf Virchow. Prostate cancer and other pelvic and abdominal cancers can infiltrate Virchow's node, making its palpation an important part of a patient's physical exam. But cancer cells can actually lodge in lymph nodes anywhere along this chain.

As I mentioned in the previous section, once the prostate cancer cells enter the arterial blood supply, they travel to all parts of the body. While these cancer cells cannot grow in most of these tissues, once they enter a tissue they can then invade its lymphatic drainage. This is most likely the reason why some men have prostate cancer in lymph nodes remote from the prostate gland. For example, I have seen prostate cancer in the lymph nodes behind the right clavicle, in the mesentery attached to the bowel (a fan shaped fold of tissue that tethers the bowel to the back of the abdominal wall) and in the nodes in the right and left armpits. When we find lymph nodes in the abdomen or elsewhere, but none in the pelvis, we call them "skip metastases."

Using The ProstaScint Scan

A common way to assess how far cancer has spread before performing radical prostatectomy is to remove the pelvic lymph nodes. But there are three disadvantages to this approach. First, removing the pelvic lymph nodes is an invasive procedure that can impair lymph drainage from the legs. Second, this procedure doesn't sample nodes near the sacrum or in the back of the abdomen—areas to which prostate cancer frequently spreads. Third, the thoroughness with which the lymph nodes are removed depends on the skill of the surgeon and the time he is willing to invest in the procedure: it is rarely complete. And it would certainly be valuable to know if your cancer spread to these other nodes: if it has, that may alter your doctor's treatment approach. And it would change how we'd follow your case after surgery or radiation in order to detect recurrent cancer in as prompt a fashion as possible. The big question then becomes: how can we detect prostate cancer in the lymph nodes without having to subject men to invasive surgical procedures? The CT and MRI scans are widely used for this purpose, but studies have repeatedly demonstrated that these techniques do a very poor job of detecting lymph node metastases. When CT and MRI scan results are compared with biopsy results, we find that these imaging techniques only identify 15–30% of known metastases: Not a very impressive number.

Alternatively, the ProstaScint scan uses an antibody that binds to the PSMA—the protein attached to the surface of prostate cancer cells. This

ProstaScint antibody carries a radioactive isotope that effectively marks the nodes riddled with cancer. In the randomized controlled trial that led to its FDA approval, the ProstaScint scan identified close to 80% of known cancerous nodes compared with only 15% for CT and MRI.

A number of issues have prevented the ProstaScint scan from wide acceptance as means for determining prostate cancer spread to the lymph nodes. One of the most troubling has been the appearance of the "skip metastases" we just dicsussed. Many prostate cancer physicians think these skip metastases aren't actually real—a sort of false positive. As ProstaScint scan use has increased, images have been produced that suggest cancer has spread to nodes in the abdomen and beyond without first spreading to the pelvic lymph nodes. One study by Gerald Murphy showed such lesions in just over 20% of patients. These findings are very controversial. In several studies, researchers removed abdominal lymph nodes because they suspected prostate cancer had spread there, only to find out later, after microscopic evaluation, that a significant proportion were actually cancer-free. For example, Cleveland Clinic investigators found a high proportion of false positives (see Ponsky, et al. in the References & Notes section in the back of this book). I confronted this issue when my ProstaScint scan showed an abnormal lymph node in the back my abdomen. After the folks at Johns Hopkins removed more than 20 lymph nodes, we found that none were actually cancerous.

You may well ask how this happens. Well, it's possible for even an experienced pathologist to miss cancer in a lymph node. RT-PCR studies have clearly established prostate cancer cells in the lymph nodes that appear cancer-free through the microscope. Edelstein, et al. from Boston University School of Medicine used RT-PCR to scan a series of lymph nodes that appeared pathologically cancer-free. The RT-PCR detected cancer in 44% (sixteen cases). Of these sixteen cases, fourteen men developed recurrent cancer within five years after surgery. So it's possible that a portion of the lymph nodes that the ProstaScint scan deemed positive and microscopic examination labeled negative actually contained cancer that the pathologist simply missed.

I also think it's important to acknowledge that there are two generations of the ProstaScint scan. Most of the negative studies revolve around the first generation scan. Dr. Sodee from Case Western Reserve markedly improved this approach by quadrupling the resolution of his scans. These much clearer images are then fused with a CT scan so that the ProstaScint positive areas are assigned to a specific lymph node or tissue. In my experience, Dr. Sodee's approach significantly improves the value of the ProstaScint scan. I have repeatedly seen this new approach identify metastatic prostate cancer in men we'd thought were candidates for surgery or in men we suspected were at risk for recurrent prostate cancer after surgery or radiation. When this recurrent prostate cancer is then treated, patients' PSAs can become undetectable, indicating remission.

Lymph Node Staging

Of the imaging techniques available, the CT scan and MRI do so poor a job that it's difficult to justify their continued use for prostate cancer lymph node staging. The one positive thing I can say is that they will detect massive involvement of a lymph node, usually only when more than one billion cancer cells are present at one place. The first generation ProstaScint scan was also difficult to perform well and in less-than-expert hands it often yielded confusing results. The second generation ProstaScint scan coupled with CT fusion is much more reliable and clearly superior to CT and MRI.

Laparoscopic pelvic lymph node dissection is regarded by many as the gold standard, but has several limitations. First, there is always the chance that the lymph nodes left behind may be the nodes that contain cancer. Second, the RT-PCR studies have clearly shown that standard microscopic examination of the lymph nodes can miss small amounts of prostate cancer. Third, there is always the risk that there may be cancer in the abdomen or chest nodes even if there aren't any in the pelvis.

So, the bottom line is that all of these techniques have limitations and all underestimate the true extent of lymph node spread in men with newly diagnosed prostate cancer.

Chapter 4
Understanding Hormonal Therapy

It is an unfortunate fact that in some circles, just like Rodney Dangerfield, hormonal therapy gets no respect. However, the clinical trials show that hormonal therapy can be an extremely effective treatment for prostate cancer at various disease stages. Yet there are more misconceptions about hormonal therapy than any other area of prostate treatment. For the most part, these misconceptions paint a pessimistic picture of hormonal therapy's effectiveness and often lead to an unfounded sense of hopelessness in many patients. These misconceptions often lead patients to avoid effective methods of controlling their diseases. But *why* are there so many misunderstandings about hormonal therapy? Well, I think the problem has its root in the fact that the pace of prostate cancer research has been so overwhelming that it is impossible for any one physician to keep up with everything published on the disease. Physicians tend to read only those prostate cancer papers that directly relate to their own specialty. In other words, surgeons tend to read about advances in surgery, radiation therapists about radiation, and medical oncologists about chemotherapy. Unfortunately, while each of these specialties administer hormonal therapy, none make it a central focus of their practice.

Two Common Myths About Hormonal Therapy

#1 Responses Only Last 18 months

This is one of the more persistent myths in the field and I can't understand how it gained such wide circulation among patients and physicians. As far as I can tell, the idea dates from a paper published in 1989 by David Crawford. Crawford conducted a large, randomized controlled trial comparing Lupron alone to Lupron + Flutamide (Eulexin).

The patients on this trial had been diagnosed with prostate cancer prior to the advent of PSA screening and therefore had more advanced prostate cancer than generally seen today. Dr. Crawford and his colleagues classified patients according to whether they had advanced, moderate, or minimal disease according the standards of that time. Those with advanced disease had widespread bone metastases and suffered from significant symptoms. On average, these patients became resistant to hormonal therapy after just over 8 months. Those with moderate disease had cancers that spread throughout the skeleton, but did not have any symptoms. These patients became resistant to hormonal therapy after an average of 18 months.

I think the common assumption that hormonal therapy lasts 18 months comes from the results seen in the patients with what was then considered moderate disease—or widespread bone metastases without symptoms. But there are many reasons why it is

Average Time to Hormonal Therapy Failure

(Point in time when half the patients have developed advancing disease)

Widespread metastases and symptoms	8-9 months
Widespread metastases, no symptoms	18 months
Bone metastases, pelvis, lower spine	4-5 years
Lymph node metastases prostate in place	7-8 years
Lymph node metatstases, prostate removed	50-95% @ 10 years *(Depends on the number of lymph nodes involved)*

inappropriate to generally cite this statistic. First, even in 1989, 18 months was just the average. In Crawford's study, half the patients continued to respond after 18 months and a significant percentage were responding at 5 years. I think it's important for patients with widespread bone metastases to know that there's a chance their cancers may continue to respond to hormonal therapy even after the oft-cited 18-month mark. Still, time and again, I see men arrange their financial affairs with the assumption that they won't live another five years only to find themselves impoverished when they're lucky enough to beat the 18-month figure. But there is no reason you *have* to have the average result!

The second problem with the 18-month figure is that I see it quoted to men who do not have widespread bone metastases. Some physicians even cite the figure to men who only have lymph node metastases or even simply a rising PSA post radical prostatectomy or radiation therapy. Of course, these patients don't have nearly as extensive prostate cancers as those in the Crawford study and are likely to continue to respond to hormonal therapy for many years to come. The table on the previous page lists our best guess of the *average* duration of hormonal therapy responses for patients with metastatic prostate cancer of various degrees of severity. Again, remember there are always patients who do much better than these averages.

Why do patients with lymph node metastases do so much better if they've had their prostate gland removed? The best study to shed light on this issue is one from MD Anderson Cancer Hospital published in 1994 by Zagars, et al. In this study, patients with lymph node spread were placed on hormonal therapy and followed until they recurred. (Note that these men did not have their prostate glands removed.) Once a patient recurred, researchers recorded where hormone-resistant disease emerged. In more than half the cases, hormone- resistant disease first emerged in the prostate gland. I think this makes sense. Hormone-resistance is the result of a mutation, a change in the genetic material in the cell, which allows the prostate cancer cell to grow at very low testosterone levels. In general, mutations are random events that occur once in every 1-10 million cells.

Thus, all other things being equal, you would expect hormone resistance to emerge at locations where there are a large number of cancer cells. (At the time of diagnosis, patients with lymph node metastases still usually have the largest bulk of cancer in their prostate glands.) If the prostate gland is an important source of hormone resistant prostate cancer, then removing the prostate gland should improve hormonal therapy's results. And indeed, at the Mayo Clinic, Horst Zincke makes it a practice to remove the prostate glands in those patients with lymph node metastases.

His results represent a dramatic improvement in the duration of hormonal therapy response. A randomized controlled clinical trial published in 1999 by Edward Messing confirms the Mayo Clinic results. (See table(s) below.)

Since 1989, PSA screening has revolutionized the field of prostate cancer diagnosis and treatment: we're diagnosing cancers earlier and earlier.

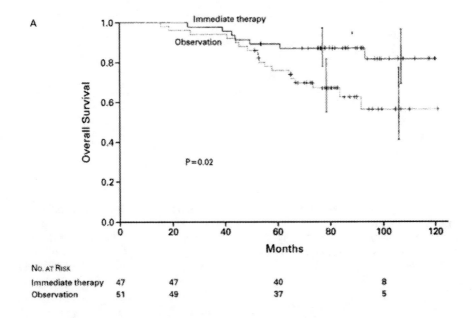

A

P=0.02

No. at Risk				
Immediate therapy	47	47	40	8
Observation	51	49	37	5

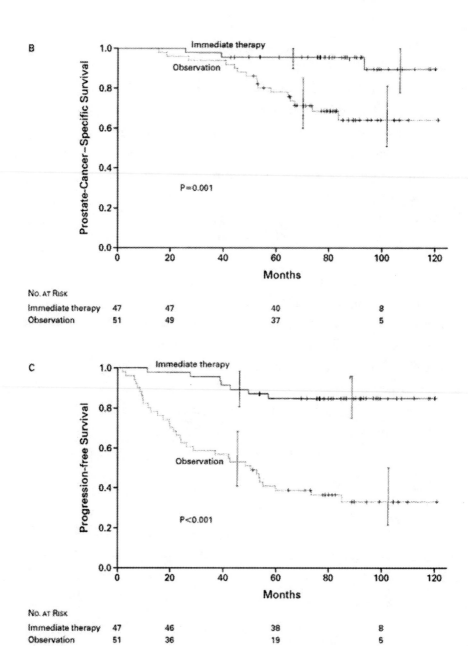

In this study, men with known lymph node metastases were all subjected to radical prostatectomy. Half of the patients were placed on Zoladex hormonal therapy within three months of surgery. The other half were given no treatment until metastatic disease appeared. This trial confirms the findings reported earlier by Zincke et al. (Reprinted from *New England Journal of Medicine*; 341:1781-1788, Dec 9, 1999).

In most studies of PSA screening, widespread metastatic disease is often identified only in the first and sometimes the second year of the screening initiative, but thereafter an overwhelming majority of patients have cancers that appear to be confined to the prostate gland.

In fact, the worst situation you are likely to see with any frequency is patients with disease that has extended to the prostate capsule, seminal vesicles, or pelvic lymph nodes. Even these patients can be treated successfully with hormonal therapy combined with aggressive external beam radiation therapy + radioactive seed implantation, called brachytherapy.

What this means is that more often than not, a man considering hormonal therapy has a PSA increasing after surgery or radiation therapy and metastases too small to see with a CT or MRI scan. We have no published series that accurately reports response duration in these patients, but I suspect that they would do as well or better than those with documented lymph node metastases after surgical removal of the prostate gland. Indeed, one series has been presented in abstract form, but not published. Drs. Scardino and Scher reviewed their experiences at Memorial Sloan Kettering in New York City and found that half of their patients were still responding at the 10-year mark. Based on my clinical experience, this result looks to be approximately correct.

My conclusion is that hormonal therapy is far more durable than generally thought. In fact, almost all men who recur after radical prostatectomy or radiation therapy will continue to respond to hormonal therapy after five years and about half will continue to respond after ten years.

#2 Hormonal Therapy Doesn't Kill Prostate Cancer Cells

Over the last several years, a growing number of patients tell me they've been told that hormonal therapy doesn't kill prostate cancer cells, but just stops cancer growth and artificially lowers the PSA test, thereby fooling us into thinking cancer cells have actually died. I find this myth very strange. Time and again, hormonal therapy clinical trials have reported shrinkage of measurable prostate cancer metastases. Depending on the clinical trial, up to 30% of patients enter complete remission, which means that all detectable prostate cancer has disappeared! How can you enter a complete remission without having killed prostate cancer cells? On the other hand, it is certainly true that some patients do not respond to hormonal therapy and among those patients, hormonal therapy hasn't killed a significant number of prostate cancer cells. It is also true that the PSA test can be deceptive during hormonal therapy. With the drop in testosterone that follows Lupron, Zoladex, Eligard or Trelstar administration, PSA values often decline to below 0.05 ng/ml by the third month. If you look carefully at the extent of the cancer at that point, you may see little or no change in the size of the cancer in the prostate gland, lymph nodes, or other sites. Instead, the size of the cancer at these sites gradually decreases over a period of many months, often taking 9-12 months to reach maximum shrinkage. However, it is true that a rapid and dramatic fall in the PSA is a good thing and indicates that the patient is a good candidate for subsequent, equally dramatic cancer shrinkage.

Chapter 5
How Hormonal Therapy Works

The concept behind hormonal therapy is that prostate cancer cells depend on the male sex hormone, testosterone, to both grow and survive. Actually, prostate cancer cells respond to both testosterone and dihydrotestosterone, hormones called androgens. Testosterone and dihydrotestosterone freely cross the outside membrane of the cell and enter the fluid inside, called the cytosol. In this fluid, there's a small protein called the androgen receptor that will bind to either of the two androgens. The receptor and the androgen to which it is bound then move into the nucleus of the cell where they bind to the genes that control growth and survival of the prostate cells. If the receptor-and-androgen combination is not available to bind to these genes, the prostate cells first stop growing and then gradually die.

What happens to testosterone and dihydrotestosterone in men on hormonal therapy? Prior to hormonal therapy, testosterone levels usually range from 400 to 800. Within 4-8 weeks after Lupron (or equivalent) administration testosterone levels fall to 10-30. Similar changes occur following surgical castration. Where does the remaining testosterone come from? The adrenal gland generates chemical precursors of testosterone, such as androstenedione, and releases these into the blood. Many tissues in the body, including prostate cancer cells, have the capacity to convert these precursors into testosterone.

Thus, standard forms of hormonal therapy *reduce* but *do not eliminate* testosterone.

Dihydrotestosterone

I can find no published studies in which researchers have measured dihydrotestosterone after medical or surgical castration. But in our clinic we find that while some may experience a decline in dihydrotestosterone of greater than 80%, many don't experience a decline at all. Since dihydrotestosterone is a much more powerful hormone than testosterone, it is certainly possible that dihydrotestosterone levels that remain within the normal range might limit the response to hormonal therapy.

When you look at the prostate cancer that grows despite this dramatic suppression of testosterone, you will still find the androgen receptor present and fully functioning. When these cancer cells are removed from the patient and tested in the lab, you nearly always find that testosterone is still needed for growth. But it may only take 1/10 to 1/1,000 the normal testosterone level to fully support cancer growth! Thus, prostate cancer doesn't become independent of testosterone, but rather becomes so efficient at using testosterone that the small amount remaining after medical or surgical castration is sufficient to support growth. How is this accomplished? One of the more common mechanisms involved is that the cancer cell makes a lot more androgen receptor. This is like using a large sail in a light wind. By increasing the amount of androgen receptor, the cancer cell makes it more likely that it will be able to bind enough testosterone to support growth. The other common change is that phosphate is added to the androgen receptor. This chemical change makes the receptor much more efficient so that fewer receptors and testosterone are needed to fully support cancer-cell growth.

Measuring Testosterone & Dihydrotestosterone Blood Levels

Frequently men come to my clinic after having failed treatment with Lupron or similar drugs, like Eligard, Zoladex, and Trelstar. These drugs aren't perfect and they don't suppress testosterone in every man. The first step in treating a man who's failed Lupron treatment is to measure his testosterone and dihydrotestosterone blood levels. You would be surprised how often we find that there's enough of either testosterone or dihydrotestosterone to fully explain why the treatment has failed. I find it very puzzling that most urologists don't measure testosterone in their patients and that nearly all fail to measure dihydrotestosterone. If the goal of treatment is to lower androgen levels, it seems obvious to me that you should measure androgen levels to make sure the drugs are working.

When you go on a diet, you measure your weight. When you depress the gas pedal on your car, you look at the speedometer. So, when you are trying to treat cancer by suppressing testosterone, you check to see that the drugs are doing what they should. This is not rocket science. If Lupron doesn't do the job, often switching to one of the competing products *will* get the job done. Surgical castration is another option. The final option is to prevent the remaining testosterone from binding to the androgen receptor through the use of drugs that compete with testosterone for its receptor.

In the previous section, we discussed how a prostate cancer that progresses after Lupron is still dependent on testosterone and outlined the various mechanisms the cancer cell uses to grow despite low testosterone levels. It turns out that in nearly every paper published on this subject, researchers added Casodex and subsequently showed that it prevented low levels of testosterone from supporting cancer growth. The concentrations of Casodex used are similar to those obtained in patients who received 150–250 mg of oral Casodex per day. I can find only one clinical trial that has tested this.

Brown, R.S., et al. biopsied the metastatic cancer masses that continued to grow despite medical or surgical castration and tested for androgen receptor content. In those patients in whom the cancer appeared to be making an abnormally large amount of androgen receptor, Casodex caused a response in 80% of the patients.

Since I opened my clinic—the American Institute for Diseases of the Prostate—in 2002, I've made it a practice to measure dihydrotestosterone levels in each patient we see. And I have to tell you that medical castration, while effective in reducing testosterone from the normal range of 300-800 ng/dL to below 30 ng/dL, often leaves dihydrotestosterone levels within the normal range (30-80 ng/dL).

Dihydrotestosterone is ten times more powerful than testosterone at stimulating prostate growth, so a dihydrotestosterone of 30 ng/dL is potentially as powerful as a testosterone of 300.

Dihydrotestosterone formation can be blocked in most patients with either Proscar or Avodart, with Avodart being more consistently effective. I've found this can aid in inducing remission in patients who've failed Lupron. Luckily, Proscar and Avodart don't cause any additional side effects in men on hormonal therapy. But again, we have to measure dihydrotestosterone levels to see if Proscar or Avodart are in fact suppressing dihydrotestosterone.

Chapter 6
Intermittent Hormonal Therapy

All of the the mentioned considerations play a role in my current approach to hormonal therapy, which is based on intense intermittent hormonal therapy (IHT). My approach integrates all I've learned about how hormone-resistance develops and aims to minimize treatment side effects. There seems to be no controversy about the fact that IHT results in a higher quality of life for men with prostate cancer compared with continuous treatment. Truth be told, I'm concerned with continuous hormonal therapy's impact on the other diseases common in men of this age group. Androgen deprivation causes a decrease in arterial compliance and an increase in insulin resistance. The change in arterial compliance fosters the development and progression of systolic hypertension and a widened pulse pressure. The increase in insulin resistance causes weight gain and exacerbates hyperlipidemia. I think it very likely that a long-term study of men on continuous hormonal therapy will show it increases heart attack, stroke, and diabetes mellitus.

While IHT improves a man's quality of life and very likely reduces potentially life-threatening complications of hormonal therapy, doubts persist about whether it is as effective as continuous hormonal therapy in controlling prostate cancer. Existing lab models consistently show that IHT delays the onset of hormone resistance and improves survival. At present, only one small, randomized controlled trial compares IHT with continuous treatment (de Leval, et al). At the three-year mark, only 7% of those on IHT were hormone-resistant compared with 38.9% of those on continuous treatment (p=0.0052). My own conclusion is that IHT is preferable because it is certainly less toxic and at least as effective as continuous treatment.

Dr. Robert Leibowitz reports excellent results with thirteen months of Lupron, Casodex and Proscar, followed by Proscar maintenance. In fact, the response rate Leibowitz reported is higher than that of any other androgen ablation program used to treat prostate cancer. And I have noted at my clinic that men on Lupron or Zoladex in combination with Casodex and Proscar experience a much more rapid decline in PSA, as well as a higher frequency of undetectable PSAs, suggesting the response is both more rapid and more complete. However, until someone does a randomized controlled clinical trial, we can never be sure that this more aggressive form of treatment favorably influences survival.

Many men labeled hormone resistant really just have cancers that are hypersensitive to androgen. That is, their prostate cancer has learned to proliferate maximally at testosterone levels of 1/10th to 1/1000th of that normally present. Mechanisms involved can include increased expression of the androgen receptor, as well as a variety of mechanisms that enhance androgen receptor activation.

Interestingly, in all of the laboratory papers on prostate cancer cells able to grow at low levels of testosterone, Casodex at levels obtained in patients after 150-250 mg a day effectively suppress tumor growth. For this reason, I recommend men with potentially life-threatening prostate cancer start on complete androgen blockade composed of Zoladex or Lupron with 150 mg of Casodex a day. By using high dose Casodex, we treat the most common mechanisms of hormonal therapy failure ahead of time.

I've also found that many men on an LHRH agonist such as Lupron or Zolodex exhibit male-pattern baldness. I often find significant dihydrotestosterone levels in these men. Adding Proscar or Avodart frequently reduces dihydrotestosterone levels to undetectable while reversing male pattern baldness as well as improving PSA suppression.

I think these observations help explain why Dr. Leibowitz obtained such a high response rate with triple hormonal blockade.

Keep in mind that Casodex can switch from an agent that blocks testosterone from binding to the androgen receptor to an agent that can bind to the androgen receptor and stimulate cancer growth. This happens when the androgen receptor and its associated proteins switch to a new configuration that now uses Casodex as if it were testosterone. This is signaled by prostate cancer progression during hormonal therapy with this agent. For this reason, a man's PSA must be followed carefully and if the results indicate cancer progression, Casodex should be discontinued and second line hormonal therapy considered. This event is not very common, but is definitely an issue that you and your doctor need to keep an eye out for.

Chapter 7
Hormonal Therapy As Adjunct

Before we move on to discuss Second Line Hormonal Therapy, I thought it best to discuss the current state of common treatments available for prostate cancer and how hormonal therapy fits into these modalities and actually improves treatment outcomes.

Radical Prostatectomy

One of the therapies that has been examined more closely the past few years is radical prostatectomy (RP). In fact, researchers have spent so much time studying RP that they have more information on it than any other treatment option for newly diagnosed patients. So it's now possible for us to have a much more accurate discussion of the strengths and limits of this procedure than we have had in the past. Most of the credit for this advance in knowledge must go to Patrick Walsh and his colleagues at Johns Hopkins. As a result of their work, we can give patients a very accurate estimate of how likely it is that surgery will control their cancer.

Prostate Cancer After Surgery

Let's begin our discussion of post-surgery recurrence with taking a closer look at the results that Johns Hopkins reports. Take a look at this table.

Postsurgery Recurrence

Men with PSA less than 0.2 ng/ml

Age(years)	5 Years	10 years	15 year
Under 50	88%	81%	69%
50-59	87%	78%	71%
60-69	84%	74%	67%
Over 70	72%	58%	58%

As you can see, with each passing year, more patients' cancers continued to grow. More than 30% relapsed by the 15th year. However, as the authors point out, a lot has changed in the last 15 years. With the advent of PSA screening, patients are diagnosed earlier in the natural history of their disease. We also do a much better job of identifying those patients with metastatic cancer than we did 15 years ago. For these and other reasons, it's likely that surgery patients today will do better at the 15 year point than those shown in the table on this page. The Johns Hopkins investigators used statistical techniques to estimate these changes and used this information to make detailed predictions of the percentage of patients likely to be in remission at various times after surgery.

Before we get into the details of this study, you need to be aware of several limitations. First, these are the results of a single institution and, for the most part, a single surgeon—Patrick Walsh. There is no guarantee that other surgeons or other institutions will match these results. Second, Dr. Walsh is well known for the strict way he limits the kind of patients on whom he's willing to operate. Other surgeons may not place such severe limits on who's eligible and who's not. This fact alone may explain why other surgeons have a lower percentage of patients disease-free at five and ten years. Finally, a team of outside investigators hasn't audited the Johns Hopkins results, so there will always be some concern that researchers did not report their results accurately. While this remark may seem a bit harsh, it's not an accident that the FDA frequently audits

Percentage of Men in Remission 10 Years Post Surgery
(Cancer confined to gland at surgery)

PSA Range	0-4	4.1-10	10.1-20	< 20
Gleason 5	99%	97%	95%	90%
Gleason 6	97%	94%	91%	84%
Gleason 3+4	92%	89%	83%	75%
Gleason 4+3	82%	77%	70%	62%
Gleason 8-10	63%	57%	52%	46%

clinical trial results before they approve a drug for marketing. Also, clinical trials sponsored by the National Cancer Institute often incorporate some form of an audit of the results. With all of these issues in mind, it is reasonable to suppose that these results are a bit on the optimistic side of real world experience.

That said, look again at the table on page 77. In the original paper, the authors also reported results for three, five, seven, and ten years. Except for those with Gleason 5 and a PSA of less than 4.0 ng/ml, all groups show a steady increase in the number of patients who have had recurrent cancer as time progressed. This fits the results reported by Hopkins and other groups—as long as 22 years after surgery, patients continue to relapse. In other words, even though a patient has remained cancer-free for ten years after surgery, he cannot be viewed as being cured. His cancer may well return at the 15 or 20-year mark. The risk of such relapses appears to increase the higher the Gleason grade and PSA at the time of diagnosis. Thus, the results shown in Table II for ten years would likely be significantly worse at 15 and 20 years.

Also remember that these patients' cancers were confined to the prostate gland at the time of surgery. But if this were true, you may well ask, why wouldn't surgery have completely removed the cancer? How can such patients still relapse years later and what does this phenomena tell us about prostate cancer? As we discussed previously, prostate cancer cells are often found in the blood and bone marrow of the newly diagnosed. This was true in my own case. It seems that a vast majority of these cancer cells can't grow. Some die rather rapidly and others persist in a dormant state. But these cells can break their dormancy and start to grow at any time, even decades later. This phenomenon is very well-documented for breast cancer and melanoma as well as for a range of other cancers. This is actually a hot area of cancer biology research. The forces that are known to foster cancer cell dormancy include the cancer's inability to increase its blood supply (angiogenesis) as well as ongoing attacks by the immune system. A lack of key growth factors may also play a role. One of the more obvious ways to improve the results of radical prostatectomy would be to find ways of keeping cancer cells dormant.

Studies show that men with Gleason grade 6 or below do well with medical management (sometimes called "watchful waiting"). It's not really clear that surgery has a significant impact on men with PSA levels below 10 ng/ml. However, I find it very interesting that men with Gleason 5 or 6 cancers do quite well after surgery even if they have PSA levels over 20 ng/ml. It's unlikely that men with PSAs this high would do as well with medical management as they have done after surgery at Johns Hopkins. Certainly, how to manage patients with Gleason 6 or below remains controversial. Dr. H. Ballentine Carter from Johns Hopkins is currently conducting a very important clinical trial that should help resolve this issue. In this trial, Dr. Carter has identified a group of men with cancers, which combine low Gleason grade and small cancer size, that look as if they represent latent prostate cancer. Carter followed these men carefully and operated only if there was significant clinical evidence of cancer progression.

As a result, he's shown that many men haven't yet needed surgery. For those who have, there was no evidence that waiting had had an adverse impact on the surgery's success.

Another really surprising result of Dr. Walsh's study was how well men with Gleason 8-10 did after surgery if they were lucky enough to have organ-confined disease. While many men with high Gleason scores have metastatic disease at the time of diagnosis, PSA screening has allowed early diagnosis. Thus, doctors can diagnose aggressive cancers early enough to allow effective treatment. Several years ago, Peter Scardino speculated that such patients were particularly likely to benefit from early diagnosis and aggressive treatment. The Johns Hopkins results appear to strongly support that contention. Radiation oncologists have also studied this patient population in an important clinical trial conducted by the Radiation Therapy Oncology Group (RTOG). RTOG showed that adjuvant hormonal therapy (hormonal therapy started at the same time or just after radiation) significantly improved radiation therapy's effectiveness in Gleason 8-10 prostate cancers. Keeping in mind the RTOG and Johns Hopkins results, it's apparent that a clinical trial comparing surgery alone versus surgery + adjuvant hormonal therapy may well provide interesting results. It may well be that with early detection, aggressive surgery, and adjuvant hormonal therapy, a high percentage of men with aggressive cancers may still be in remission at ten years.

Over the past few years, there've been a growing number of articles in medical journals and the mainstream press that have argued that PSA-screening and any other means of early detection cause more harm than good. Many argue that PSA-screening leads to an increase in the diagnosis of prostate cancers that don't really need to be treated because their slow growth rate means they don't pose a threat to a patient's survival or even his quality of life. Now, when I read articles like this, I think it's apparent that the authors are really thinking of the typical Gleason 5 or 6 cases, where such a controversy actually does exist. But these articles ignore the existence of small, but very aggressive prostate cancers, which are the ones most likely to kill a patient. The table below shows, in a very dramatic fashion, the impact early detection and treatment can have on these dangerous cancers.

If I were a urologist and wanted to extend the value of radical prostatectomy, I would focus on high-grade prostate cancer treated with surgery and the most effective adjuvant therapy I could find. I would also aggressively identify and treat any other medical conditions likely to limit a patient's lifespan.

Gleason 8-10
The Importance of Early Detection & Aggressive Treatment
(Percentage in remission at 10 years)

PSA Range	0-4.0	4.1-10	10.1-20	< 20
Organ-Confined	63%	57%	52%	46%
Not Confined	21%	15%	11%	7%

Lymph Nodes & Surgery

Many surgeons won't do a radical prostatectomy when they find there's cancer in a man's lymph nodes. They assume that surgery isn't a viable choice because there's no longer a chance that the operation can remove all of the prostate cancer. Radiation therapists have similar concerns. There was a period of time when I also agreed with this viewpoint. But a number of studies have changed my opinion.

In 1994, Zagars, et al. from MD Anderson Cancer Center published treatment results for a group of men with cancerous lymph nodes but no detectable cancer in their bone. The men received hormonal therapy rather than surgery or radiation. After ten years, most of the men had failed hormonal therapy. Investigators then took the important step of finding out where in the body hormone-resistance first appeared. In more than half the cases, hormone resistance appeared first in the prostate gland. In somewhat more than 40% of the cases, hormone resistance appeared in the bone and in less than 5% of cases in the lymph nodes. The implications of this study are very provocative: even after lymph node metastases developed, the cancer remaining in the prostate gland is still the biggest threat to the patient's continued health.

So then what happens if we operate on men with lymph node involvement? The largest series of patients treated in this fashion are those from the Mayo Clinic under the care of Dr. Zincke. For more than 20 years, Dr. Zincke has treated such men with radical prostatectomy followed by hormonal therapy. And over the years, he's written many papers detailing his results. Overall, his patients do extremely well. Since he treated a large number of patients, he can provide a great deal of detail on how the lymph node involvement affects his results. At one extreme, men with only one node have a 95% chance of being in remission at ten years. As the number of abnormal nodes and amount of cancer increases, the chance of being in remission drops to almost 50%. Other factors also alter success rates. If the cancer has a normal number of chromosomes (diploid), hormone resistance is quite uncommon regardless of the extent of lymph node spread. A cancer with an abnormal number of chromosomes (aneuploid) tends to do much worse.

One randomized controlled trial (published in 1999) tested Dr. Zincke's approach. In this study, surgeons operated on all men with known lymph node metastases. Within three months after surgery, half of the men started hormonal therapy with Zoladex alone. After a median of seven years, close to 80% of men on combined treatment were in remission compared with 18% of those who'd only had surgery. And less than 10% of those on combined treatment died compared with more than 30% of those treated with surgery alone. This trial has been criticized because it was terminated early for the difficulty researchers had getting the ideal number of patients into the trial. I think this criticism misses the point: the differences were astoundingly positive for combined treatment and are consistent with the MD Anderson paper that represents a dramatic confirmation of Dr. Zincke's claims.

Furthermore, these results are consistent with laboratory studies of prostate cancer in animal models and make sense in terms of what we know about prostate cancer biology.

So, at this point, I think there's a strong case for using radical prostatectomy to treat men with lymph node—but not bone—metastases if you follow surgery with adjuvant hormonal therapy. Of course, controversy remains about the best way to administer hormonal therapy. In particular, it may well be that intermittent hormonal therapy will prove to be both more effective at cancer control and less toxic to the patient. However, this sequence of studies clearly shows that hormonal therapy is effective in treating lymph nodes with a large enough volume of cancer to be seen on a CT scan. It does not seem much of a stretch to think that hormonal therapy would also be useful against prostate cancer metastases too small to be seen on a CT scan.

Radiation Therapy

Radiation therapy technology has advanced rapidly over the past 10 years. Currently, randomized controlled trials that followed men treated with radiation alone or combined with hormonal therapy for long enough to provide significant survival statistics used now obsolete techniques. Older studies that addressed various aspects of this problem are RTOG 85-31, 86-10, and 94-13, as well as EORTC 22863. Taken together, these studies show that adding hormonal therapy reduces the risk of cancer recurrence in the prostate gland as well as at distant sites, such as bone, but that the impact on the prostate cancer death rate ranges from modest to nonexistent. In any case, the trial results compare poorly with Zincke's reports and with those of the confirmatory randomized controlled trial conducted by Dr. Messing. In the end, all we can do is guess about modern radiation therapy's impact.

That said, I do think it's certainly plausible that advances in radiation therapy would improve results. 3D conformal radiation and IMRT make it possible for radiation therapists to deliver doses in excess of 75 Gray (7,500 cGy or rads in the older literature). Zelefsky, et al. from Memorial Sloan Kettering demonstrated that we can now deliver doses in excess of 80 Gray with mild side effects. Roach, et al. at University of California, San Francisco showed they could safely boost the dose to 90 Gray for the portion of the prostate gland containing the largest amount of cancer. Prior to these technical advances, it was difficult to reach 70 Gray and many radiation therapists wouldn't go above 65 Gray. This is important because the effectiveness of radiation therapy increases rapidly as the radiation dose moves from 70 to 75 Gray. In a recent paper Howard Sandler estimated that for each 1 Gray dosage increase, relapse risk decreased 8%. The end result is that it's now possible to deliver a radiation dose to the prostate gland and the immediate surrounding fatty tissue sufficient to sterilize the cancer. As a result, in men with localized prostate cancer, the best radiation therapy series shows equal to or better control than radical prostatectomy results. So there's really no doubt that radiation therapy done with 3D conformal or IMRT effectively treats cancer within the prostate gland.

Of course a natural question then becomes what role adjuvant hormonal therapy may play. Earlier studies showed that one of adjuvant hormonal therapy's benefits was that it reduced the frequency of recurrences within the prostate gland. In other words, it converted inadequate doses of radiation into more effective treatment for cancers within the prostate gland. With the higher radiation doses now possible, there is less of a need for hormonal therapy to aid radiation control of cancer in the prostate gland.

Lymph Nodes & Radiation Therapy

Recent advances have also altered how we use radiation therapy to treat possible pelvic lymph node metastases in men with high-risk prostate cancer. A major factor limiting radiation therapy's effectiveness in treating possible pelvic lymph node involvement was simple positioning: the small bowel is quite close to some of those nodes. Any accidental radiation to the small bowel can cause potentially catastrophic gastrointestinal injury. This limited the amount of radiation that could be delivered. But with the recent advances in radiation therapy, radiation therapists can deliver higher doses to the lymph nodes—although usually not as high as the dose we can deliver to the prostate gland itself. Radiation therapists can now treat the pelvic lymph nodes with radiation doses in excess of 50 Gray, which is sufficient for adjuvant treatment, but not for large volume lymph node disease. Radiation therapists can also treat the nodes next to the prostate gland with radiation doses that approach or exceed 75 Gray and can easily treat portions of the cancer that protrude from the gland.

At this point I think the radiation therapist is better able than the surgeon to deliver effective treatment to prostate cancer that's outside the gland but still confined to the pelvic area. But the radiation therapists still have difficulties delivering large enough doses to sterilize the lymph nodes with massive cancer deposits. There are a few non-randomized controlled trials that illustrate what we can and can't do with radiation therapy. Dr. Michael Dattoli published results he obtained using aggressive radiation therapy with 3D conformal radiation and radioactive seed implantation for men with locally advanced prostate cancer and poor risk features. Overall, 79% of his patients had a PSA at or below 0.2 ng/ml at ten years. Many of these men were at high risk for pelvic lymph node spread. Dr. Critz had similar results with his outcomes from using 3D conformal radiation plus radioactive seed implantation to treat a group of men with high risk prostate cancer: just over 60% had a PSA at or below 0.2 ng/ml at ten years.

After reviewing these results, though, I naturally asked myself if adjuvant hormonal therapy would improve either Dattoli's or Critz's results. Both the surgical studies mentioned earlier and the older randomized controlled radiation therapy trials suggest that hormonal therapy effectively treats cancers even modern radiation therapy techniques can miss: i.e., cancers that have spread to the bone and to the lymph nodes outside the pelvis. We've discussed how prostate cancer can frequently enter the blood stream and spread throughout the body. We've also talked about how it can invade bone marrow. The cancer cells at these sites receive no radiation treatment and represent a potential source for cancer metastases. In the surgical series we reviewed earlier, relapses commonly occurred ten to fifteen years after prostatectomy. In the existing randomized controlled trials, adjuvant hormonal therapy consistently reduces the rate at which distant metastases develop. From everything I know about the biology of prostate cancer, it certainly seems that controlling distant micrometastatic cancers remains a problem for men who receive modern, more intense radiation treatment to their prostate gland and to other pelvic sites of disease spread. For all of these reasons, I think that adjuvant hormonal therapy still has an important role to play. It offers the potential to increase radiation control of large lymph node metastases and it provides additional control over distant micrometastases.

However, there are virtually no published randomized controlled clinical trials that test the benefit of combining adjuvant hormonal therapy with the best of modern radiation therapy. So it's certainly possible that advanced 3-D conformal and/or IMRT techniques have increased the effectiveness of radiation sufficiently to eliminate the need for adjuvant hormonal therapy. I know that some radiation therapy experts believe this. But I highly doubt this is true: prostate cancer can spread early to areas radiation can't reach—to the lumbar spine via the venous plexus in the pelvis, for instance, or to the lymph nodes over the sacrum and in the abdomen. For all of these reasons, I think men with high-risk disease undergoing radiation therapy should continue to use adjuvant hormonal therapy. This practice should only stop when well-run clinical trials clearly demonstrate that it's no longer needed.

In the end, I come away from reviewing radiation therapy literature with the sense that the whole issue of adjuvant hormonal therapy combined with radiation needs to be reexamined. We need a new generation of clinical trials comparing IMRT techniques with and without hormonal therapy. And, actually, this is really not very different from the situation I faced in 1999 when I had to choose my own treatment.

My current approach is quite conservative. I continue to steer men with lymph node metastases or men at high risk of developing it to centers equipped with the most modern radiation therapy available while also recommending adjuvant hormonal therapy. Similarly, I think using adjuvant hormonal therapy after surgically removing the prostate gland represents a reasonable approach. Hormonal therapy alone is not the best course of action for men with these types of cancers, primarily because Zagars' study demonstrated such a high risk for developing hormone-resistance in the prostate gland, which, as we mentioned earlier, is a greater risk to one's life.

Metastases & Hormone Resistance

When I see a patient who failed hormonal therapy and who may be a chemotherapy candidate, I make it a practice to determine the location and amount of cancer first. This is the common practice in medical oncology we discussed earlier called staging. As we have just discussed, while the CT scan is able to identify lymph node metastases in about 15 to 30% of cases, the ProstaScint scan does so in 80%. This is why I order ProstaScint scans with CT fusion for many men, as it nicely combines the benefit of both techniques. As I've done this over the past three years, I've been surprised to find that a number of men have only a single cluster of cancerous lymph nodes. We've had great success using radiation or surgery to remove these cancer deposits. As a result, instead of having to face chemotherapy, these men find themselves with an undetectable PSA. It remains to be seen how durable these responses will be, but at the very least these men have an opportunity to go off hormonal therapy or avoid chemotherapy for a period of time.

Chapter 8
Second Line Hormonal Therapy

There's actually a class of drugs called second line hormonal therapy agents, which we traditionally use when the treatments we discussed in earlier chapters fail. Over the past five years, there's been a steady evolution in the use of these agents that make them much more effective. (I find it interesting how a series of small changes in treatment can often mean significant benefit for patients.)

Ketoconazole

Ketoconazole effectively suppresses adrenal androgen production, but also directly kills hormone refractory prostate cancer. In patients who've failed initial hormonal therapy, a standard approach is to initiate ketoconazole. This drug not only blocks adrenal androgens effectively but is also active against hormone refractory prostate cancer. In a well-done clinical trial, Eric Small showed that ketoconazole has a 50% response rate in hormone refractory prostate cancer, making it the most active single agent in that setting. Physicians traditionally used Ketoconazole in doses of 400 mg every eight hours. But this dose is associated with significant nausea, vomiting, malaise, and liver damage. Dr. Small shows that by reducing the dose to 200 mg every 8 hours, side effects are markedly reduced without compromising the drug's effectiveness as a prostate cancer treatment.

Ketoconazole impairs the synthesis of steroids like cortisone. At the dose of 200 mg every 8 hours, ketoconazole doesn't cause any problems if a man's stress level—emotional or physical—is low. But given the trauma of a major illness and the emotional, physical, and financial stress a cancer diagnosis can bring, many men may develop adrenal insufficiency. For this reason, I typically give patients replacement hydrocortisone at doses of 20 mg each morning and 10 mg each evening.

Ketoconazole has a short half-life and needs to be administered every 8 hours by the clock. Additionally, it is only absorbed effectively from the stomach when under acidic conditions. For this reason, we recommend that the drug be taken with an acid beverage, such as Coke, Pepsi, or a fruit juice. The only exception to this is grapefruit juice. Grapefruit juice blocks a protein found in the gut and liver called CYP3A4. This protein is involved in destroying half of all prescription drugs, including ketoconazole as well as antibiotics like erythromycin, statins used to lower cholesterol, and many other drugs as well. In general, you should not take grapefruit with any prescription drug unless it is specifically cleared by your doctor.

The final issue which makes the use of ketoconazol complex is that like grapefruit juice, ketoconazole also blocks CYP3A4 and similarly the drug interferes with the body's ability to clear half of all prescription drugs. This means that before ketoconazole starts, your doctor needs to review all of the drugs you are taking to see if there is a possible problem. It also means that you cannot start any new drug without first having your doctors check to see if it interacts with CYP3A4. These are all factors that need to be taken into consideration before starting treatment.

Estrogen

One of the earliest treatments for prostate cancer involved giving men estrogen, the female sex hormone. In fact, doctors were already using it by the 1950s. At that time, estrogenic agents like diethylstilbestrol (DES) were administered orally and clearly caused major responses. Researchers thought that these drugs caused responses because they reduced testosterone blood levels, but the truth is a little more complicated. While estrogenic drugs do suppress testosterone levels, they also directly kill prostate cancer cells by binding to estrogen receptor beta in these cancer cells. Thus, estrogenic drugs can be very effective in men who no longer respond to testosterone blockage. This form of treatment fell out of favor because a randomized controlled trial showed that oral estrogens caused severe cardiovascular side effects that killed almost as many men as they saved. These side effects include high blood pressure, fluid retention, blood clot formation in the legs, and pulmonary embolism. Recently, several investigators noted that modern cardiovascular disease management allows many of the side effects of oral estrogenic drugs like DES to be safely resolved. For example, we now have diuretics that reduce fluid retention and antihypertensives that reduce blood pressure. Even low dose coumadin can effectively reduce blood clot risk. We also have a better understanding of how estrogenic drugs work.

But there's also a major controversy surrounding which form of estrogen to use and how to best administer it. As I mentioned, the traditional approach is to give oral estrogenic drugs such as DES. Transdermal estradiol has been extensively studied in women, where it appears to have many advantages over oral estrogen. Compared with the oral route, there is no first-pass exposure to the liver and this reduces liver production of clotting factors, thereby reducing blood clot risk. There are numerous other advantages.

Transdermal versus Oral Estrogen

Liver Protein Target	Adverse Effect	Oral	Transdermal
Angiotensin precursor	Salt retention Hypertension	Increase	No increase
C-reactive protein	Arteriosclerosis Stroke	Increase	No increase
Suppress IGF1	Muscle loss	Exacerbate	No effect
Clotting proteins Pulmonary Embolism	Blood clots	Increase	No increase

Transdermal estradiol may be the best way to administer estrogenic drugs to men with prostate cancer. A recent clinical study published by Ockrim, et al, in *Journal of Urology* confirmed that transdermal estradiol is a safe and effective way to administer estradiol to men with prostate cancer and can cause very significant anticancer activity. It certainly appears to be safer than oral estrogenic drugs such as DES.

There are a number of issues that remain to be resolved. For example, how many estrogen skin patches are needed to get the best response? Is transdermal estrogen the best way to give estrogen? Or might it be better to inject a slow release form of estrogen? (This is, in fact, available and may prove much more convenient than the skin patch.)

We also use transdermal estradiol to suppress hot flashes: a patch that delivers 25 mcg of estrogen a day is often sufficient to reduce hot flashes and will often cause only minor breast symptoms.

A final advantage of transdermal estrogen is that it is much less expensive than any other form of hormonal therapy.

Sandostatin

Sandostatin suppresses growth hormone production and is therefore usually used to treat people with acromegaly, a disease caused by too much growth hormone in adults, and giantism, a disease caused by too much growth factor in children. Around the globe, there are several different anti-growth hormone drugs on the market, but in the

United States, only Sandostatin is available. Throughout the rest of this section, I will will discuss the drugs in this family as if they are interchangeable, which I believe to be the case.

Growth hormone plays a potential role in how hormone resistance develops. Growth hormone causes another hormone to be released—insulin like growth factor I or IGF1. As many of you probably already know, IGF1 plays a very important role in prostate cancer biology. First, it triggers a major survival pathway for prostate cancer by activating a protein called akt. Akt is important because, once activated, it causes many changes in the cancer cell that make it much more resistant to hormonal therapy, chemotherapy, and radiation therapy. IGF1 also activates pathways that may cause the androgen receptor to function at the low levels of testosterone seen in men who are medically and surgically castrated. So there's actually a possibility that simply suppressing growth hormone could reverse hormone resistance. This is not a new idea and it has been around since the early 1990s. But it's difficult to identify the right way to use this information and how to best design appropriate clinical trials to test the concept. To my mind, the investigators at the University of Athens Department of Urology have done the most convincing work in this regard. In a series of papers, they show that Sandostatin-like drugs, when combined with a steroid called dexamethasone, appear to restore hormone sensitivity to hormone resistant men. This led to a randomized controlled trial that compared chemotherapy with a Sandostatin-like drug + dexamethasone that found the Sandostatin-like combination as effective as chemotherapy in terms of response rate, response duration, and ultimate survival. Of course, Sandostatin is much less toxic than chemotherapy: about the only side effect is diarrhea during the first month of treatment and mild fatigue. To date, I've had limited experience with the University of Athens protocol, but their results are favorable enough to convince me that this is an important addition to our golf bag.

Leukine

Leukine is the brand name for the hormone GM-CSF, or granulocyte macrophage colony-stimulating factor. Leukine is interesting because this is a hormonal treatment for prostate cancer that has nothing to do with testosterone. The major defense against infection involves activating the white cells in the blood. These white cells include a wide range of different cell types that act together to fight off viral, bacterial, and fungal infections. These same cells also appear to play a role in the immune response to cancer cells. GM-CSF stimulates a wide range of white cells involved in the defense against infection and antitumor immunity. It does this by increasing the number of white cells as well as their biologic activity. Leukine is approved for use with chemotherapy to prevent infections. Physicians also use it in patients whose bone marrow transplants have not taken well because it can lessen the risk of infection.

While Leukine, or GM-CSF, is normally used to reverse low white blood counts caused by chemotherapy, it also improves host immune response to cancer. Experimentally, it has been used to enhance cancer vaccines' ability to generate a therapeutically effective response. It is also used to expand dendritic cells used by cancer vaccines, such as the Provenge vaccine developed by Dendreon. Clinically, subcutaneous Leukine administration can reduce the risk of melanoma recurrence following surgical removal of the original tumor. With this background in mind, Eric Small (Rini, et al) at UCSF reported his experiences using Leukine to treat a group of advanced prostate cancer patients. In a paper published in *Journal of Clinical Oncology*, Small reported that Leukine could slow or even arrest prostate cancer progression. The schedule used in Small's study was every day for 14 days out of every 28. Since the study's publication, I've treated a number of patients with Leukine and have pretty much confirmed what Dr. Small reports.

Furthermore, patients tolerate this treatment quite well. That said, patients can also get a transient inflammatory reaction at the injection sites as well as edema. But both side effects reverse within 72 hours if we stop drug administration. Over the counter antihistamines, such as Claritin, are quite effective in lessening the severity of these side effects.

Leukine also appears to have useful activities far beyond infection and cancer immunity. A recent study in Crohn's disease suggests that the 14-day schedule may not be optimal: patients treated daily for 8 weeks had side effects comparable to that seen in the 14-day schedule. With this extended schedule of administration, about half of Crohn's disease patients go into remission.

Finally, I should mention that Leukine has a number of other interesting therapeutic effects, including reversing damage to the gastrointestinal tract caused by radiation and chemotherapy and the reversal of coronary artery disease.

Combining Second Line Hormonal Therapy Drugs

Since ketoconazole, estrogen, Leukine, and Sandostatin each attack the prostate cancer cell in a different way, it is possible that these agents might be used in combination with each other or with other agents used to treat prostate cancer. Since these agents have very different side effects, it is also possible that patients will tolerate combinations of these agents quite well. We are only beginning to see clinical trials testing such combinations. For example, Eric Small presented an abstract at an ASCO meeting that tested ketoconazole + Leukine and found the combination resulted in a response rate of 78% and was well tolerated. I have also repeatedly used ketoconazole and transdermal estradiol together and found them very effective in treating hormone resistant prostate cancer, even after chemotherapy has failed. Patients also tolerated it very well. Adding Sandostatin (because it blocks a major survival pathway for prostate cancer) may increase the response to many other agents that act to kill prostate cancer, including ketoconazole and estradiol as well as chemotherapy. Such uses represent an important area for future study.

As you can see, you're not just playing golf with a driver and a putter. Unlike twenty years ago, there are many options available to today's prostate cancer patient which provide the hope and optimism patients need to actively treat, survive, and thrive with a high quality of life after prostate cancer.

Chapter 9
Case Studies

While some people learn by studying the game intensely before they even pick up a club, others find it useful to learn as they play. We have included a number of case studies here that nicely illustrate the various game strategies that can be applied to treating prostate cancer. Keep in mind that these cases are only anecdotal and I have formulated my strategies here not only to put the cancer in check and bring down the PSA but also to keep an eye toward patients' overall health. After all, what's the point of curing the cancer if the patient dies in a month of heart disease or some other chronic illness.

Case Study #1: XD

XD's case nicely illustrates many of the issues that make treating men who have advanced disease at the time of diagnosis so complicated. In the process of trying to get XD into complete remission, my staff and I at the American Institute of Diseases of the Prostate (AIDP) ended up using all of the tools we've discussed in this book: aggressive androgen withdrawal, ketoconazole, transdermal estrogen, Leukine, and even taxotere-based chemotherapy. But don't look at this case as a course for your own treatment: at AIDP we individualize each treatment path to fit a patient's specific overall medical condition. For example, XD had significant arteriosclerosis leading to the placement of stents in his coronary arteries right in the middle of prostate cancer treatment. This altered my approach and from that point on we had to adapt to the aggressive heart treatment recommended by his cardiologist—or in other words play around this obstacle with an eye for the bigger picture.

In September 2003, XD made an appointment with his urologist when he began to have symptoms of urinary tract obstruction. The urologist quickly noted that XD's prostate was abnormally enlarged and subsequently checked his PSA, which proved to be 1,026 ng/ml. Transrectal ultrasound and biopsy of the prostate gland revealed a Gleason 4+4=8 prostate cancer that involved both sides of the gland. A CT scan showed clear involvement of the lymph nodes along the iliac arteries on both sides of his pelvis and in the nodes along the back of his abdomen. A bone scan showed a hot spot in his left scapula.

We started XD on Zoladex plus 50 mg of Casodex toward the end of August. When I saw him close to three weeks later, his PSA had dropped to 69 ng/ml. I increased his Casodex to 150 mg per day and added Proscar. Thirty days later, his PSA had dropped to 3.7 ng/ml. By December 10, his PSA reached its lowest point (1. 42 ng/ml) and then began to increase, indicating failure of initial hormonal therapy. I prescribed ketoconazole, Leukine, and 0.2 mg per day of transdermal Estradiol. By March, his PSA reached 0.76 ng/ml and again began to increase. At this time, he developed chest pain that proved to be secondary to partial blockade of two coronary arteries. We had to stop cancer treatment until these blocked arteries were opened up again using stints. From this time on, he was also on Plavix and baby aspirin. By the end of April, his PSA had again increased, this time to 1.08 ng/ml. I placed him back on ketoconazole and Leukine and his PSA decreased to 0.4-0.45 and remained in this range.

Prior to the onset of XD's cardiac problems, it became clear that we wouldn't attain a complete remission with ketoconazole and Leukine. For this reason, we suggested he go on chemotherapy. He began chemotherapy with Taxotere and high dose Calcitriol. He didn't respond to this treatment: his PSA increased gradually from 0.40 to 0.62 ng/ml. He'd tolerated taxotere remarkably well, with almost no side effects. (Taxotere is eliminated from the body by a liver protein called CYP3A4 and some people have high levels of this protein, leading to rapid destruction of Taxotere. Interestingly, this same protein appears in prostate cancer cells when they become resistant to taxotere.)

At that point, I switched him to a combination of Taxotere and Navelbine and re-introduced Leukine. Note that I was still concerned about a possible CYP3A4 problem. But a single ketoconazole pill per day can block CYP3A4 without adding any significant risk. For this reason, I put XD on 200 mg of ketoconazole once a day. On this program, his PSA dropped to 0.13 by the end of January 2005, but did not decline further. In February 2005, I decided to stop further chemotherapy. At this point, I increased his Leukine from 250 mcg 14 days out of every 28 to 500 mcgs a day. XD continued taking Zoladex and Proscar. Over a few weeks, his PSA dropped to 0.10-0.11 and remained there until August 2005. Two years after his diagnosis, I decided to stop hormonal therapy and didn't administer his routine Zoladex shot. He switched from Proscar to Avodart, because his dihydrotesterone was not as low as I would have liked. He remained on Leukine. Over the next several months, his PSA dropped to 0.04 ng/ml and has remained there. (To put this PSA in perspective, a successful radical prostatectomy will yield a PSA below 0.04-0.05 ng/ml.) At this point, we obtained a bone scan and CT scan that found no evidence of prostate cancer. Thus, after a long and complex treatment course, this patient is now in complete remission. Our next challenge will be to keep him in complete remission. We both hope Leukine and Avodart will do the job.

Case Study #2: AP

At age 53, AP was diagnosed with prostate cancer. Prior to diagnosis, his only PSA test was a 1.9 ng/ml from 1995. In September, he had a PSA drawn as part of a set of routine blood tests. The result? 3,488 ng/ml. His doctor repeated the PSA seven days later and got a result of 3, 905 ng/ml. The doctor then biopsied AP's prostate gland and discovered that AP had a Gleason 4+4=8 cancer. A

CT scan revealed severe lymph node involvement in his left pelvis. Cancer had also spread to the lymph nodes at the back of his abdomen. Luckily, though, bone scan showed no evidence of prostate cancer.

AP's form of prostate cancer is relatively uncommon: it spread widely throughout his lymph nodes without involving bone, lung, or liver. Patients like AP often enjoy an excellent, sometimes dramatic, response to hormonal therapy that can continue for years.

Almost immediately, AP started on Lupron and Casodex at 50 mg per day. (He started taking both drugs on the same day.) Four days later, his PSA had increased to 4,000 ng/ml.

This response isn't unusual. Lupron will actually increase testosterone and stimulate cancer during the first 4-7 days. It only significantly suppresses testosterone in the second week. This is called the Lupron Flare. We usually administer 50 mg of Casodex for four days to one week prior to initiating Lupron or similar drugs like Zoladex, Eligard, or Zometa in order to block this "flare." Alternatively, doctors administer 150 mg of Casodex the day of or day before Lupron treatment starts. This is called a "loading dose" and gives blood levels within a few hours that would take weeks to achieve with 50 mg of Casodex.

AP then proceeded to see a number of medical oncologists who made recommendations ranging from immediately starting taxotere chemotherapy to treatment with Lupron alone.

AP arrived at my clinic door about one month after he'd started Lupron. After our evaluation, I told him that because he had only lymph node and not bone or organ involvement, there was a chance that he might have a dramatic response to hormonal therapy, but that the hormonal therapy should be more aggressive. For this reason, I changed his treatment to include 150 mg of Casodex and 0.5 mg of Avodart. This is typical "triple hormonal blockade." I added Fosamax at 70 mg per week to reduce osteoporosis risk and ursodiol 300 mg twice a day to reduce liver damage risk from Casodex.

I also suggested he get his PSA checked monthly. If his PSA stopped falling, I said I would switch him to second line hormonal therapy with ketoconazole and/or transdermal estradiol. We also discussed Leukine with both AP and his wife. If Leukine didn't cause a further decline in his PSA, we planned to switch him to taxotere chemotherapy. But AP responded very well to treatment and his PSA fell to below 0.01 ng/ml within ten weeks of starting treatment.

By the end of six months of treatment, no cancer could be detected by CT scan and I declared him in complete remission. He is now on Leukine and Transdermal estradiol to consolidate this remission and I plan to take him off all hormonal therapy within several months.

Based on other cases I've seen and on the published literature, AP is most likely to develop hormone resistant disease in his prostate gland. The second most likely site would be bone. We have discussed the possibility of radiation therapy to his prostate gland to reduce the risk of hormone-resistant disease at that site, but AP wants to continue on the current medical management plan.

AP's case illustrates the fact that some forms of prostate cancer can be very responsive to hormonal therapy, especially if there are no bone metastases.

Case Study #3: BK

BK was diagnosed with prostate cancer in December 2000 when he was admitted to the hospital for acute kidney failure. The cause of the kidney failure? A very large prostate cancer had blocked urine drainage through his ureters: the tubes that take urine from the kidney to the bladder. A biopsy revealed a Gleason 4+4=8 prostate cancer. His PSA was 3,656 ng/ml. He started on Lupron with a short course of Casodex to prevent the Lupron Flare discussed in AP's case. BK's physicians told him his life-span would likely be short, but they would help him die with dignity. He then had a transurethral resection of the cancer that was blocking the flow of urine from the bladder. By March of 2001, his PSA had declined to 12.3 ng/ml. By January of 2003, his PSA had reached 0.86 ng/ml and he stopped Lupron.

By June of 2003, six months after stopping Lupron, BK's PSA had increased again, this time to 14.2 ng/ml. He started on Lupron, again with Casodex administered beforehand only long enough to block the Lupron Flare. This time, the PSA reached its lowest point on October of 2003 at 1.37 ng/ml and then started to increase despite continued Lupron. For this reason, his doctors started him back on Casodex and his PSA fell to 0.23 ng/ml by August of 2004.

In October of 2004, I saw BK for the first time. I remember thinking this was quite a story because here it was five years after presenting with a PSA of greater than 3,000 ng/ml and kidney failure and he was really in great shape overall with just a few problems that needed to be addressed. In my judgment, his main problem was that he had had an incomplete response to hormonal therapy. Also, he had been on hormonal therapy for much of the previous five years with no attempt to prevent osteoporosis. Of course, kidney failure also promotes loss of bone. So, it was not a surprise when we discovered he did indeed have osteoporosis. I told BK that I would prefer to go for a complete remission. BK, however, had already confronted the issue of dying from prostate cancer and was more philosophical about the situation. He wanted to control his disease, but only if it didn't compromise his quality of life.

Of course, I respected him and his decision.

The least toxic form of hormonal therapy I know is transdermal estrogen, but in this particular setting, it is not likely to cause a complete remission. However, it was the treatment that best fit his needs. As a benefit, transdermal estradiol would markedly stimulate new bone formation, thereby treating his osteoporosis. To this end, I added transdermal estradiol to his current treatment. After a short period, BK decided that even this program was more intrusive on his quality of life than he wanted and he stopped all treatment except for Proscar in February 2004 with a PSA of 0.33 ng/ml. He did agree to do eight weeks of Leukine, which he tolerated but which did not have any impact on his disease.

By November 2005, his PSA had increased to 6.7 ng/ml and he agreed to start transdermal estradiol alone with the goal of treating his disease with minimal side effects. At this point, I also tried to establish how much cancer remained in his body and where the cancer was located. Dr. Bruce Sodee at Case Western Reserve did a ProstaScint scan with CT fusion that showed BK had cancer only in his prostate gland. All lymph node disease had disappeared and he had no bone metastases. I told him that there was a chance that radiation therapy to the prostate gland might put him into complete remission for many years and might cause a permanent remission. After thinking about this option for many months, BK decided that he did not want to risk the side effects of radiation therapy.

On his current treatment, BK's PSA declined over six months until it reached a plateau between 1.8 and 2.3 ng/ml. At this point, summer was just around the corner and, since BK planned to enjoy a Cape Cod retreat, he elected to stop treatment.

BK is yet another dramatic illustration of how prostate cancer that spreads widely to only the lymph nodes can respond very well to treatment that is much less than optimal. I find it astounding that six years after presenting with a PSA of greater than 3,000 ng/ml and kidney failure, the only cancer we can detect is limited to the prostate gland and he is living nearly a normal life. I only hope I can eventually convince him to go for a complete remission while his cancer is still confined to the prostate gland.

Case Study #4: ZQ

ZQ was diagnosed with prostate cancer in 1994 with a PSA of 35 ng/ml. While his Gleason score was 5, a laparoscopic lymph node biopsy revealed lymph node metastases. For this reason, he was refused a radical prostatectomy. Instead, ZQ went through multiple cycles of triple hormonal blockade consisting of 12 months of treatment followed by several years on Proscar, and then Avodart when it became available. In July of 2001, he was in an off phase of hormonal therapy when his PSA increased to 0.36 ng/ml; he then restarted Lupron. While ZQ's PSA initially declined to 0.8 ng/ml, it then started to increase.

When I saw ZQ in September 2002, his PSA had gradually increased to 0.43 ng/ml while still on Lupron. At this point, I added Casodex at 150 mg a day. I also asked him to get a bone scan and ProstaScint scan to determine the extent of his disease. These scans revealed a cancer limited to the prostate gland and nodes in the left obdurator chain. These lymph nodes are in the pelvis and are accessible to radiation therapy, particularly through the skilled use of IMRT. In March and April of 2003, ZQ received radiation treatment to those nodes and to his prostate gland. At that time, I switched him from Casodex to low dose ketoconazole (200 mg every 8 hours) because I felt it would be more effective in consolidating the remission induced by radiation of the pelvic lymph nodes.

BQ then stopped taking Lupron and ketoconazole by December 2003. He remains on Avodart at the time I wrote this profile (June of 2006). His PSA has remained at or below 0.08 ng/ml for two years and seven months after the end of hormonal therapy. His main remaining problem is that he became obese during those many years of intermittent hormonal therapy and needs to lose 34 pounds if he is to remain free of cardiovascular disease.

ZQ's case shows several interesting characteristics. Gleason 5 prostate cancers are noted for being slow to grow and spread. This was apparent from his treatment history in that his PSA increased only gradually off hormonal therapy. This phenomena was revealed in a spectacular fashion by the bone scan and ProstaScint scan done in 2002. Here he was 8 years after a diagnosis of metastatic prostate cancer, yet his cancer had not spread beyond a single lymph node group. Radiation therapy had advanced dramatically between when his 1994 diagnosis and when we discovered the limited extent of his disease in 2002. ZQ was able to undergo effective treatment because our ability to visualize and treat prostate cancer had advanced so dramatically in the intervening eight years.

Chapter 10
Diet & Lifestyle

Since we are one of the few groups who emphasize diet and supplements as a critical part of prostate cancer management, I'm going to go into the details of what I recommend and why. Let me say that I think it is difficult to obtain durable complete remissions in metastatic prostate cancer with any frequency if you ignore diet and supplements. Also, as I discuss below, hormonal therapy leads to insulin resistance and this fuels weight gain as well as an increase in blood pressure and serum lipids. The diet I'll discuss is now well established as an effective approach to both insulin resistance and hypertension. It will help minimize the damage hormonal therapy may cause to your general health. For these reasons it is important to understand the impact of diet on prostate cancer treatment. First things first: I am a medical oncologist and as such I have a vested interest in the impact various agents can have on cancer cells. In many ways, what you eat and the vitamins you take can have as much influence on creating a curative treatment program as hormonal therapy or whatever treatment or combined treatments you choose. In this section I've included the vitamins and supplements necessary for a successful hormonal therapy plan.

Hormonal Therapy & Weight Gain

Men undergoing androgen withdrawal, either by surgical castration or through the use of drugs such as Lupron, Trelstar, Zoladex or Eligard, usually gain 5 to 20 pounds. This weight gain is often associated with worsening blood lipid levels, including both cholesterol and triglycerides. At the same time, this weight gain is also associated with an increase in blood pressure. Blood pressure measurements include two numbers and it is the top or systolic number that increases the most during hormonal therapy.

What is going on here? It appears that low testosterone levels make insulin less effective. This insulin resistance is the same basic defect that leads diabetics to crave carbohydrates and to overeat. Insulin resistance leads to the development of what is now called the Metabolic Syndrome. This syndrome is characterized by elevated blood sugar, elevated serum triglycerides, systolic hypertension and an increase in body fat, particularly in the abdomen. Needless to say, these things are not good for your health. This is especially true if you already have metabolic syndrome, diabetes, hypertension, high blood lipids or a history of heart disease.

This information has a number of implications. First, before you go on hormonal therapy, you need to have a complete physical exam and preexisting diseases just discussed should be treated. Your family doctor or cardiologist need to know that these problems may get more difficult to manage while you are on hormonal therapy.

But the truth is that you may be able to dramatically reduce or eliminate this cardiovascular risk. In fact, the same lifestyle and dietary changes that are good for your general health will also act to limit the damage hormonal therapy can cause.

America is in the midst of an obesity epidemic that has the same consequences as the insulin resistance caused by hormonal therapy. As you might expect, prevention or reversal of insulin resistance is a hot research topic these days. In this chapter, we will review the impact of diet, exercise and medications that help you minimize this problem.

Mediterranean Diet

I currently recommend that all patients go on a Mediterranean, heart-healthy diet. While there are now clinical trials that show a benefit to a low fat vegan diet, these are too strict for most patients. The Mediterranean diet is much easier to adopt.

But the Mediterranean diet shouldn't be considered in isolation, but rather as a part of a healthy lifestyle. While the details of a healthy lifestyle are well known, one recent study did an outstanding job of putting this all into perspective. The article was published in the Journal of the American Medical Association and was a report of the HALE project. In this study, 2,339 Europeans from 11 countries between 70-90 years of age were followed between 1988 and 2000. This paper analyzed the impact of four health practices on 10-year survival: not smoking, moderate alcohol consumption, exercise, and the

Mediterranean diet. Both moderate alcohol consumption and the Mediterranean diet reduced death rates by 23% and 24%, respectively. Exercise and not smoking were more effective and reduced deaths by 37% and 35%, respectively. The combination of all four health habits reduced deaths by 65%! Remember, the people in this trial were already elderly. Imagine what the impact of these four practices might have if they were started earlier in life?

Most people in America and Europe die of cardiovascular disease and cancer. If you are reading this book, you most likely already have prostate cancer and the odds are high that you also are on the road to heart disease, whether you know it or not. How did these lifestyle changes mentioned in the study alter the risk of dying of each of these common diseases? Those who followed all four healthy lifestyle options had a 67% drop in the risk of cardiovascular disease, which includes stroke, peripheral vascular disease, heart disease, etc. For coronary atherosclerosis, the death rate dropped by an impressive 73%. Overall cancer death rates dropped by 69% and all other causes of death by 67%. These are simply astounding numbers and all achieved without a single penny spent on prescription drugs or pills filled with herbs. No wonder *Forbes* magazine recently called a healthy lifestyle the single largest threat to drug company profits!

By now, I am sure you are all anxious to hear the details of how you can gain these amazing health benefits. It turns out to be very simple. I suppose I do not need to say much about not smoking. If you don't smoke now, don't start. If you are smoking, there are many resources available to help you stop.

That's the first step. The rest of the lifestyle changes require a bit more discussion.

Second, you need to drink the equivalent of one or two glasses of wine each day. In this study, they did not analyze different forms of alcohol separately, but other studies have. All alcoholic beverages show some heart benefits, but red wine does seem somewhat better. In this study, they found that the specific amount was not particularly important.

Third, you need to exercise at least 30 minutes each day. It need not be intense and could be nothing more than walking or gardening.

Fourth, you should consider adopting the Mediterranean diet. In America, this is very easy because the ingredients are readily available because the state of California has a Mediterranean climate and very productive agriculture. There are a number of excellent cookbooks available to guide you in this transition. The principles of this diet are relatively simple. The major fat in the diet is olive oil, which owes its health-promoting properties to its rich content of monounsaturated fat. Other monounsaturated oils can also be used, such as almond, macadamia, hazelnut and avocado. In addition to these oils, legumes, grains, and nuts contribute most of the calories and protein. Fruits and vegetables fill out the bulk of the diet without adding very much to the total caloric content. Limited daily consumption of diary products, in the form of cheese and yogurt, is also common and supplement the protein content of the legumes and grains. Eggs, fish, shellfish and white poultry are consumed several times a week. Red meat, including pork, is only consumed occasionally during the month.

While the Mediterranean diet was the subject of this study, it is not the only diet that can promote longevity. The Asian equivalent of the Mediterranean diet would be the Okinawan diet. This diet has attracted interest because the Okinawans are the longest-lived human population. This diet has many similarities to the Mediterranean diet in that grains (rice) and legumes (tofu) combined with vegetables and fish form the bulk of the diet. As with the Mediterranean diet, red meat is not commonly used. The major difference is that the Mediterranean diet has a much higher fat content because of its extensive use of olive oil and nuts.

As you can now see, we outline a very simple, easy-to-understand approach to optimal health. Four simple lifestyle changes can reduce America's death rate by more than 60% over a 10-year period, even when applied late in life.

Obesity & Prostate Cancer

Plus, being obese may actually increase your risk of getting progressive prostate cancer, especially developing hormone-resistant prostate cancer. Numerous investigators have already reported an association between obesity and adverse outcomes for prostate cancer patients, but this area remains mired in controversy. Still, there is increasing evidence that some of the hormonal changes triggered by obesity may fuel cancer growth.

Research has identified a range of new hormones that regulate eating and getting fat. One of the best studied of these is leptin. Scientists discovered leptin when they developed of a strain of mice with a genetic predisposition to obesity. These mice don't produce the protein we now call leptin. When this strain of mouse is injected with leptin they lose a significant amount of body fat, confirming that it was the original lack of leptin that led to obesity. Later, researchers showed that leptin is produced by fat cells in increasing quantities as they fill with lipid. The result is that gaining body fat increases production of a hormone that further limits fat production by decreasing feeding and other metabolic changes. In contrast, fasting caused a rapid decrease in leptin production in mice.

For a while, it looked as if leptin injections might be an effective way to treat obesity, but this hope waned as it became obvious that leptin did much more than reduce body fat. Obesity is associated with increased inflammation of the arteries and other tissues. And the most convenient measure of this inflammation is the ultrasensitive C-reactive protein test (CRP). An elevated CRP result has now been shown to be as important as the serum total cholesterol count in predicting who is at risk for heart disease. And we now know that leptin stimulates inflammation by releasing a protein called tumor necrosis factor (TNF) and a protein called IL-6. (It is now thought that many of the adverse consequences of obesity are the consequences of chronic elevation of leptin.)

Both leptin and IL-6 stimulate the growth of human prostate cancer and elevated blood levels of either protein are associated with a poor prostate cancer prognosis. In particular, leptin stimulates the growth of hormone-resistant prostate cancer. Thus, leptin is directly or indirectly linked with obesity, inflammation, cardiovascular disease, and prostate cancer progression.

In human beings, calorie restriction leads to a rapid drop in blood leptin levels as well as levels of TNF, IL6, and CRP. As I just noted, the most successful programs for weight loss all incorporate diet and exercise. Research has repeatedly shown that exercise reduces circulating leptin, TNF, IL6, and CRP. The longer you exercise, the more your blood leptin levels decrease. In fact, exercising for more than one hour appears to be necessary for maximal reduction. Ultramarathoners, or runners who compete in races up to 50 or 100 miles, carry this process to the ultimate and very dramatic suppression of leptin.

Why I Favor The Mediterranean Diet

There is now very powerful evidence in support of the Mediterranean Diet as specific treatment for heart disease. Perhaps the most important study is the Lyon Diet Heart study. In this clinical trial, 605 people in the intensive care unit with their first myocardial infarction were randomized either to a typical Northern European diet with modest restriction in cholesterol and fat versus a Mediterranean diet patterned after that typical of the Island of Crete. Over a four-year time period, the patients on the Mediterranean diet had a greater than 50% decline in their risk of a second heart attack as well as a range of other adverse events, such as stroke.

They also experienced an equally large reduction in their risk of cancer.

In the aftermath of the Lyon Diet Heart study, many investigators have looked in greater detail as to why this diet may have such a beneficial impact on general health. One key finding is that this diet markedly improves insulin resistance and many manifestations of the Metabolic syndrome. This may come as a surprise to many Americans who view the Mediterranean diet as the equivalent of having a large plate of spaghetti for dinner and thus very high in carbohydrates. In fact, this is far removed from the diet of the Mediterranean. In fact, it is a high fat diet with between 30-40% of calories coming from fat. However, instead of a cheeseburger and French fries, the fat comes from the olive and its oil as well as a range of nuts like almonds, pistachios and hazelnuts. Fatty fish also contributes to fat content of this diet. The fats found in the Mediterranean diet are largely monounsaturated or rich in omega 3 fatty acids. In contrast, the American diet is rich in saturated fat and omega 6 fats. Again, there is a large and growing literature on why this difference in fat type is so important.

Protein sources are also quite different. Red meat is consumed once every 2-4 weeks, while fish and poultry tend to be weekly. On a day-by-day basis, much of the protein comes from grains and legumes (beans and lentils) supplemented with dairy products.

Unlike American dairy products, in the Mediterranean area, especially Crete, the diary products are produced by sheep and goats grazing on grass and brush rather than grain-fed cows. Milk produced from grass- and brush-fed animals has a very different fat composition than that from grain fed animals. The latter is lower in saturated fat and omega 6 fats.

Another key factor is that fruits and vegetables play a central role in the Mediterranean diet. Many of the greens we use today are inherited from the food culture of the Mediterranean area. Lettuce, spinach, radicchio, broccoli, and beets all come to us from the Mediterranean basin. Fruits include apricots, plums, apples, figs, and pomegranates. However, the dominant fruit of the region would have to be the wine grape. The consumption of wine is not only a hallmark of this diet but apparently important for cardiovascular health.

You may well ask why the Mediterranean diet is so healthy. The complete answer is unknown. However, this diet has many properties that would seem to contribute. We have already discussed how the kind of fat found in this diet tends to be quite different from the typical American or Northern European diet in that it is low in saturated and omega 6 fat and high in monounsaturated and omega 3 fats. The Mediterranean diet is also a much richer source of antioxidants: the fruits and vegetables are all rich sources, but so are olives and olive oil.

In addition to the fact that this diet may well help you limit the damage caused by hormonal therapy, it may well help limit the progression of your cancer. Saxe et al. looked at a group of men who had failed surgery and now had progressive prostate cancer. When these men were placed on a Mediterranean diet similar to that used in the Lyon Diet Heart study, PSA doubling times were reduced by greater than 60%. In the laboratory, chemicals found in red wine, such as resveratrol, suppress the growth of prostate cancer. In one study, drinking red wine reduced the risk of high-grade prostate cancer by more than 60%. There is even one small recent study that found drinking pomegranate juice slowed the progression of prostate cancer. So, while you are minimizing the damage hormonal therapy is causing to your health and waistline, you may also be doing something that may slow the progression of your cancer.

Exercise

Men on hormonal therapy tend to lose muscle strength and muscle mass. While this obviously limits what you can do physically, it very likely contributes to the weight gain and exacerbates the insulin resistance. If you adopt a program of aerobic exercise and resistance exercise, you can limit your loss of muscle strength and muscle mass and your recovery from hormonal therapy, once it has stopped, will also be more rapid.

Aerobic exercise can be as simple or as elaborate as you want to make it. At a minimum, you should aim for at least 30 minutes of brisk walking. If the weather is unfavorable, join an exercise club or walk a large indoor mall. In my own case, we got a treadmill and placed it in front of a television set. Now, even when I finish work at 9 PM, I can still get my time in.

Key Resistance Exercises

Of course, the best way to go about developing a resistance exercise program is to join a health club and have a personal trainer set up a program that incorporates the proper form and techniques. If you can't (or don't want) to do this, here are basic exercises you can do at home with inexpensive bar bells and ankle weights.

Resistance Exercises

Leg Extension
Calf Raise
Leg Curl
Chest
Chest Press
Lat Pull-down
Overhead Press
Triceps Extension
Biceps Curl
Modified Curl-up

In addition to these exercises, your weight loss program should include squats and lunges. Because these exercises involve the large muscle groups of the trunk, hips, and thighs, they play a critical role in building aerobic fitness as well as providing muscle mass to burn calories. These exercises should be done six times each in sequence. Repeat this sequence two more times. You should plan three sessions of resistance exercises a week.

Lunges

Lunges are an excellent way to tone your legs and buttocks and help you maintain good balance. Use the back of a chair or the edge of a table to help with your balance. Remember: always stay in your own comfort zone during the exercise and keep good form. Move slowly and smoothly.

When your thigh strength increases, you can take the lunge lower and increase the time you spend at the bottom of the movement. When you are stronger and more stable, try holding 3- to 5- pound weights in your hands as you lunge. Muscle groups involved are: gluteus, hamstrings, quadriceps, and calf. Make sure you do three sets of each lunge type.

1. Keep your body upright and positioned directly over your hips throughout the lunge.

2. Take one large step forward. Transfer your weight from your back foot to your front foot.

3. Drop your back knee so that it touches the floor. You may not be flexible enough to get down this far at first; flexibility comes with practice.

4. Once the back knee is touching the floor (or as low as you can comfortably go) push backwards with your front leg until you return to the starting position.

5. Alternate between left and right legs.

6. Repeat exercise with each leg six times.

Side Lunge

This variation helps with balance, flexibility, and inne-r and outer-thigh strength.

1. Hold onto a table or chair.
2. Stand with feet about shoulder width apart.
3. Move your right leg to the right, bend your knee, and lower slightly. Repeat with the left leg.

Lunge Around The Clock

This is an advanced variation of the lunge that's especially effective at promoting balance and coordination.

1. As before, start with your feet about shoulder width apart.
2. With the image of a clock in your mind, lunge in a circle to each hour point, starting with twelve, then one, two, and so on.

Squats

Squats are a great exercise for your legs. They help build strength and stability because they build your quadriceps while also strengthening the hamstring, calf, and gluteus muscles. The stronger your leg muscles, the more endurance you'll have for walking and standing, which ultimately improves your balance.

1. Hold onto the back of a chair or the edge of a table if you feel the need to help maintain your balance.
2. Make sure your feet are wider than shoulder-width apart, with legs pointing out about 40 to 45 degrees. By placing your legs in this broad stance, you will significantly reduce the stress on your knee

joint. The more commonly used stance—knees shoulder-width apart, puts significant torque on this joint.

3. Your head should be titled back slightly, with your eyes positioned upward.

4. Keep your chest high and inhale deeply as you concentrate on dropping your hips as if you were going to sit in a chair. Go down far enough so that your buttocks are even with your knees. Hold here for five seconds and exhale as you rise back to the starting position. If you have trouble going down this far, just stop where you feel comfortable.

5. Keep your knees directly over your feet.

6. Repeat six times.

7. When you feel you need more of a challenge, try squatting with a 3- to 5-pound dumbbell in each hand.

8. Make sure to keep your eyes positioned upward—looking down can throw your balance off and make you tip forward.

Prescription Drugs & Supplements For Muscle Strength & Weight Loss

For the most part, I favor a program based on a heart-healthy diet and a reasonable exercise program. However, there is a growing list of supplements and prescription drugs that have been reported to support muscle strength or aid in weight loss.

Creatine

In muscle, creatine is converted into phosphocreatine, an important energy store for muscle contraction. There are multiple studies that document that creatine supplements increase muscle strength. Often, athletes use supplements for sports that require more speed and power. A more recent study shows that endurance athletes may also benefit from creatine supplementation because it allows them to function at a higher rate of energy output. One common dosage program for creatine calls for a six-day regimen of 5 grams daily, followed by 1-2 grams once or twice a day. Such a program offers an increase in muscle mass, muscular strength, peripheral blood flow, resting energy expenditure, and improved blood cholesterol. This increase in muscle mass and resting energy expenditure appears to result from an increase in myogenin and suppression of myostatin.

Supplement vendors advocate creatine as a means to protect and enhance brain function. These claims may well be valid. There is now a double-blind randomized controlled trial that did indeed show oral creatine had a significant impact on brain function in a group of vegetarians. Researchers chose vegetarians for this study because most dietary creatine comes from the consumption of meat. So vegetarians represent an easily identifiable group of people likely to have low dietary creatine levels. At the time of publication, I could find no evidence that oral creatine can offer meat-eaters brain function protection or enhancement, but there's also little evidence that the supplements will do any harm.

While this all makes creatine sound like a wonder supplement, there are a number of problems. First, there's a great deal of variability in how people respond to creatine. Some don't respond at all and others may have a minor benefit. The key gene involved in the human response to creatine is creatine kinase. This gene comes in multiple inherited forms; some appear to support a positive response to creatine and others do not.

A second problem is that some researchers have reported that oral creatine may increase insulin resistance, the underlying mechanism that leads to adult onset diabetes mellitus. But I'm skeptical of this observation. It makes no sense based on what we know about creatine biology and is in direct contradiction with the rest of the medical literature on the supplement.

Third, creatine increases the amount of water retained by muscle: some men may gain as much as six pounds of water during the first week or so on creatine. In contrast, increased muscle power develops much more gradually.

The bottom line is that creatine can effectively enhance muscle mass in a way that will benefit some men in their quest to build muscle mass and lose body fat. Unfortunately, there's no way to tell if you'll respond to creatine before giving it a try.

Creatine & Hormonal Therapy

As I said in the beginning of this chapter, men on hormonal therapy face added obstacles when it comes to weight gain. Men on hormonal therapy typically gain 5–20 pounds during their first year of treatment. This weight gain is often associated with increased blood cholesterol and blood pressure, along with an enhanced risk of diabetes mellitus. But the weight gain can actually obscure the magnitude of the problem because the drop in testosterone during hormonal therapy can lead to a substantial loss in muscle mass. The actual gain in body fat is often much greater than the number of pounds you've gained suggests. Muscle mass loss leads to a decline in upper and lower body muscle strength and can make you tire quite easily.

There are several things you can do about this problem. A recent randomized controlled trial showed that exercise alone effectively prevented fatigue and preserved muscle strength. But exercise without supplementation didn't do as good a job at preventing the decline in muscle mass and increase in body fat. Unfortunately, I can't find any clinical trials that examine the combination of aerobic and resistance exercise with calorie restriction and high-quality protein consumption. For what it's worth, I know several patients who've used such a program to maintain muscle mass while remaining thin. A number of those men find creatine supplementation helps them maintain muscle power.

Reductil or Meridia

The generic name for this drug is sibutramine and it is one of the more successful prescription drugs used to treat obesity. Sibutramine reduces your appetite and increases thermogenesis. You only need to take it once a day. It comes in a wide range of doses (5-15 mg), so the physician can tailor the dose to your individual needs. Multiple randomized controlled trials show the drug successfully causes a 5-8% loss in body weight. But sibutramine is significantly more effective if it is combined with a well thought out program of diet and exercise.

Patients on sibuteramine not only lose weight, but also have decreased levels of blood lipids and uric acid, the cause of gout. In diabetics, the drug improves blood sugar and reduces insulin resistance. Unfortunately, none of the clinical trials are of long enough duration to determine if the drug reduces death rates from cardiovascular disease or diabetes.

Sibuteramine enhances the action of norepinephrine, dopamine, and serotonin in the brain and this action plays an important role in suppressing appetite. Common side effects include rapid heart rate, increase in blood pressure, nervousness, and anxiety—all of which are common in drugs that enhance epinephrine and norepinephrine. One study showed that 25 mg of Metoprolol a day blocked the side effects from these hormones without affecting weight loss.

Sibuteramine is related to an earlier agent that had to be removed from the market because it damaged the heart valves and caused hypertension in the artery that supplies the lung. But by now, sibuteramine has been on the market long enough for us to know that the risk of these side effects is very low or even absent.

Nevertheless, if you have hypertention, you should only take sibuteramine if the hypertension is well-controlled and your physician is monitoring your blood pressure. You also shouldn't take sibuteramine if you're taking monamine oxidase inhibitors to treat depression, or are on any drug that enhances norepinephrine. Nor is it wise to take the drug with serotonin reuptake inhibitors like Paxil, Zoloft, or Celexa.

Sibuteramine's impact on prostate cancer patients hasn't been studied. But again, we know that in the lab epinephrine can stimulate prostate cancer cell growth. Because sibuteramine's side effects appear to be caused by epinephrine, it is possible that the drug could stimulate prostate cancer growth.

Epinephrine's action on prostate cells can be blocked by Cardura, Hytrin, and/or Flomax. But unfortunately I can't find any studies that examine the impact of these drugs on sibuteramine-induced weight loss.

The bottom line is that sibuteramine is an effective drug that can cause modest weight loss with modest side effects. But for the reasons listed above, I would only consider it for prostate cancer patients when all other approaches have failed.

Xenical or Orlistat

In the intestine, a protein called lipase breaks down fat, releasing fatty acids. This step is necessary for the absorption of most dietary fat. Orlistat blocks lipase, thereby preventing dietary fat absorption. This dietary fat remains in the gut and is then expelled in stool. There are multiple clinical trials demonstrating that Orlistat is effective in causing weight loss. But for it to work, you need to combine the drug with a low fat diet. When used in conjunction with appropriate diet modification, individuals commonly lose 10% or more of their body weight. Adding an exercise program further improves results. Carbohydrate-restricted diets are only recommended in conjunction with Orlistat if the initial low-fat diet doesn't help you lose weight.

Like sibuteramine, Orlistat improves blood lipid levels, reverses insulin resistance, and enhances sugar control in diabetes. One recent study showed that Orlistat significantly reduced the risk of diabetes in a group of obese, nondiabetic patients over a four-year period.

Because Orlistat reduces fat absorption, there's been some concern that it might impair the absorption of fat-soluble vitamins A, E, D, and K. But this doesn't seem to be true. This drug does appear to alter the absorption of other fat-soluble nutrients, such as beta carotene, lycopene, and lutein. In fact, many are also concerned that Orlisat may interfere with several fat-soluble drugs. Though only a few drugs have been studied, results to date don't show a significant decrease in their absorption.

After a high fat meal, Orlistat can cause one disturbing problem: since a lot of fat is passed in stool, there's a tendency for it to leak out through the rectum, staining undergarments. We recently reviewed the possible health benefits for beta sitosterol and polyphenolic antioxidants found in olive and avocado oils. We also discussed the overall health benefits of these monounsaturated fats. So, if you're taking Orlistat, your body wouldn't be able to reap the benefit of any of these elements. Instead, you'll have to deal with an embarrassing personal hygiene problem.

I think Orlistat is fairly safe and effective as an adjunct to a diet and exercise program for most patients. Because it doesn't cause norepinephrine-like effects, I am more comfortable with giving orlistat to prostate cancer patients than I am sibuteramine. The only negative issues may be possible poor absorption of certain fat-soluble nutrients and oily stool.

Weight Loss Drug Development

Basic research on factors that control fat accumulation and loss is progressing rapidly. This has led to the identification of promising targets for drug development. One drug that appears very exciting and is likely to be available in the near future is Acomplia or rimonabant by Sanofi-Aventis. The active ingredient in marijuana is tetrahydrocannabinol, or THC. One of the well-known side effects of marijuana use is an increased appetite. This effect of THC on appetite appears to be mediated by the impact of THC on the cannabinoid-1 receptor in the brain. While THC stimulates the cannabinoid-1 receptor, Acomplia does just the opposite and blocks this receptor. As a result, people just want to eat less. In addition to weight loss, patients on this drug experience reversal of insulin resistance and the Metabolic syndrome. There is also some suggestion that this drug might slow the growth of a variety of cancers, including breast and prostate cancer. As with any new drug, I am sure we do not yet fully appreciate all of the potential side effects that might occur, so caution seems warranted.

Vitamins & Supplements

Over the past few years, I've been asked repeatedly which supplements I take and why. In order for you to understand my approach, you need to know that I regard these supplements as drugs and use much of the same methods to evaluate them as I would a drug. In medicine, there is a broad consensus as to what constitutes proof that a drug is a useful treatment for a disease. The most powerful evidence is a clinical trial in which patients are randomly assigned to the drug or placebo. Alternatively, the randomization could be between a new drug and an old drug. These are sometimes called Phase III clinical trials. The best-randomized controlled trials include large numbers of patients followed for years. Large numbers are needed to ensure that the differences seen are not due to chance, but indeed reflect a solid reproducible difference. Duration of a study is important because, with prostate cancer, we want to make sure that the benefit is durable.

In prostate cancer treatment, we do not have nearly enough randomized controlled trials and we often have to make due with studies that are less convincing. We have many trials in which a group of prostate cancer patients are carefully characterized and treated in a consistent fashion and the results compared with what might have been expected from historical experience with similar patients. These are called Phase II clinical trials. Much of the information we have today on the impact of radical prostatectomy arises from clinical studies like this. The obvious weakness of this design is that the patients on the new treatment might have done better for some reason unrelated to the new treatment itself. For example, since the arrival of PSA-based screening there is a trend toward diagnosing patients with smaller cancers more likely to be confined to the prostate gland. It is natural for these patients to live longer after the diagnosis of cancer than patients diagnosed in the early 1980s, even if treatment had not improved at all. Similarly, improvement in anesthesiology and postoperative care might reduce complications of surgery, yet the improvement might accidentally be assigned to improved surgical techniques.

Even further down the ladder of quality would be the "clinical experience" of well-known physicians. In medicine, there is very convincing evidence that "clinical experience" is a remarkably poor guide to selecting treatments!

There is yet another source of medical information and this comes from analyzing the frequency with which various human populations are diagnosed with and die of prostate cancer. This is the field of epidemiology. The goal of epidemiology is to look for associations between various factors, such as diet or screening, and the risk of being diagnosed or dying of prostate cancer. A good example of this is the frequently quoted fact that deaths from prostate cancer are lower in Japan than in the United States. Of course, Japan and the United States differ in many ways. While diet is different, so is the racial composition of these two populations and thus their genetics. Additionally, the details of medical care and even the willingness to diagnose prostate cancer, a disease involving a male sex organ, may also differ markedly. The best epidemiologists use very sophisticated statistical techniques to identify and control for such variables. Despite these efforts, few medical experts regard epidemiology studies as proof of anything. I think their major value is to identify issues that can then be addressed more definitively in well-designed randomized controlled trials.

The final source of information would be studies that emerge from the laboratory. In my experience, this is the place where patients and some physicians make their biggest mistakes. Time and again, I will see a patient take a supplement because some study on prostate cancer cells in the laboratory suggested a possible therapeutic benefit. Overall, very few laboratory findings prove to be true when subjected to clinical trials. My best guess is that it may well be only one out of ten or twenty promising laboratory

Supplements I Recommend

Lycopene 10 mg with each meal

Selenium 200 mcgs a day

Vitamin E 200 IU a day

Fish Oil 4,000 mg a day

Soy isoflavones 200 mg a day

Vitamin D3 (or cholecalciferol) 4,000 IU a day

Supplements I DON'T Recommend

Curcumin

Milk Thistle

Resveratrol or grape seed extract *

Zyflamed

CoenzymeQ10

Ambertose

* I do recommend reserveatrol as wine or grape juice.

findings prove to be useful in the clinic. In fact, I am probably being overly optimistic. However, the problem does not stop there. Time and again, I have seen patients take a supplement at doses ten or 20 times the highest known safe dose.

What do I look for? First, I would prefer to see at least one randomized controlled trial that demonstrates a supplement to be safe and effective. There are some exceptions. If a supplement has other well-accepted health benefits and known record of safety, I will accept a well done Phase II clinical trial. As you will see, there is one situation where I have based my decision on well-accepted general health benefits and one population-based study.

With all of these rules, my list of supplements is quite short and is shown on page 147.

For your interest, I'm also listing some of the more popular supplements I do not take because I think there is not enough information to justify their use.

In the remainder of this chapter we'll discuss each supplement and the reasoning behind my recommendations.

Vitamin D

I'm starting this discussion with, and devoting most of the segment to, vitamin D because I think it is by and large the most important supplement for prostate cancer treatment. Vitamin D has become a subject of interest in both the general health field and the study of prostate health. In fact, it's rather refreshing to know that there are simple dietary changes you can make that can greatly impact your health, whether in the context of treating a potentially life-threatening disease, such as prostate cancer, or submitting to a lifestyle pattern that can potentially help you live longer and improve the quality of your life

There have been major advances in our understanding of vitamin D over the past several years. This led to a recent NIH conference on vitamin D and to many discussions on the prostate cancer web-based support groups.

The first major change is that there has been a shift in opinions about how much vitamin D people need each day. The recommended daily allowance of 400 IU was based on the amount needed to prevent rickets. Of course, these studies were done in young children, so it was a huge mistake for the powers that be to think this would be appropriate for adults! Its always a risky proposition to point to a single paper or investigator responsible for changing a field, but there's actually one paper published in 1999, in the American Journal of Clinical Nutrition by Reinhold Vieth from Toronto, Canada that's revolutionized the way I view vitamin D. In this article, Vieth stated that the current recommended daily allowance of 400 IU was inadequate. While vitamin D is well known for its ability to prevent rickets in children, it can also reduce the risk of osteoporosis, diabetes, heart disease, muscle weakness, and many other diseases. Vieth points out that humans exposed to the sun quite rapidly manufacture vast amounts of vitamin D—far in excess of 400 IU. In fact, after twenty minutes of summer sun exposure, young individuals in their 20s can produce 20,000 IU. It's also clear that people don't develop vitamin D toxicity from exposure to summer sun, so we can obviously safely tolerate much larger amounts of vitamin D than a mere 400 IU. Vieth also argued that it was unlikely that we'd have developed this capacity for vitamin D production if we didn't need it. The best current scientific understanding of this capacity is that humans are equipped to produce large amounts of vitamin D during the summer months and store the excess in our fatty tissues. These stores then act to lessen the risk of vitamin D deficiency during the winter months.

Unfortunately, most of us get much less sun than our ancestors did. Most of us no longer have to hunt or farm by hand to feed ourselves. The average American spends most of his or her workdays indoors. And once sunlight passes through a glass window, it loses the capacity to generate vitamin D in your skin. The darker someone's skin, the less vitamin D they produce for a given amount of sun exposure. Also, as we age, our skin becomes much less effective at manufacturing vitamin D during sun exposure. As a result of skin aging and reduced sun exposure, vitamin D deficiency is quite common in those over age 80. Some foods are rich in vitamin D, including fish and milk that has been fortified with vitamin D. However, many people don't eat fish and many can't tolerate dairy products. As a result, many Americans have vitamin D levels much lower than optimal.

But how much vitamin D should you take if you never get any sun? The best current estimates are 4 to 5,000 IU a day. The best estimate for those of us with routine sun exposure would be 2,000 IU. However, I should point out that these numbers are only estimates. We have no randomized controlled trials lasting long enough to fully establish how much is needed to obtain all the benefits.

What Does Vitamin D Do?

Vitamin D does not act directly. The scientific name for vitamin D is cholecalciferol. Cholecalciferol is converted in the liver to 25 hydroxy-cholecalciferol (calcidiol), which is the major form of vitamin D in the blood. In fact, calcidiol blood level is the best single measure of whether you're getting enough vitamin D. In general, deficiency is defined as a calcidiol level of less than 20-40 nmol/L. But this is far from optimal. One of vitamin D's key functions is to promote absorption of calcium from the gut; an increase in calcidiol from 20-40 nmol/L to 100 nmol/L is associated with a very significant increase in calcium absorption.

While calcidiol is the major form of vitamin D in the blood, it is not the form of the vitamin that's responsible for the health benefits listed above. The key step in this process is the conversion of calcidiol into calcitriol. Most of the calcitriol found in the blood is produced in the kidney from calcidiol. For this reason, people with severely damaged kidneys often don't have enough calcitriol to support bone health and need extra calcitriol to prevent severe bone problems. In these cases, vitamin D and/or calcidiol aren't sufficient because the individual can't convert either to calcitriol.

While most of the conversion of calcidiol to calcitriol happens in the kidneys, considerable conversion also occurs in other tissues like the skin. Calcitriol actually appears to be quite important for skin health.

Prostate Health & Vitamin D

Normal prostate cells are one of the sites where calcidiol converts to calcitriol. This is important to prostate health because when vitamin D levels are too low, the risk of benign prostatic hypertrophy or BPH rises. Why? Well, calcitriol slows the growth of prostate cells, keeping the gland normal in size.

One very interesting recent observation is that prostate cancer cells lose this capacity to convert calcidiol to calcitriol. And there's now extensive evidence that calcitriol suppresses prostate cancer cell growth. Because many prostate cancer cells do not make their own calcitriol, the only way they get exposed to the compound is through calcitriol in the blood stream. This fact explains why many epidemiology studies link calcitriol to metastatic prostate cancer risk or death from prostate cancer. In fact, Giovannucci and colleagues at the Harvard School of Public Health found that the risk of metastatic prostate cancer was significantly lower if a man's calcitriol blood level was above 40 pg/ml.

While calcitriol alone can slow prostate cancer growth in patients, this active form of vitamin D also changes the cancer in ways that make it more sensitive to other forms of cancer treatment. The most dramatic example of this is calcitriol's impact on taxotere's activity (Docetaxel). Adding high dose calcitriol one day prior to taxotere nearly doubles the response rate to this chemotherapy drug with a significant decrease in taxotere side effects.

When prostate cancer involves bone, it increases the amount of calcium deposited at the site of involvement; this increase comes at the expense of the rest of the skeleton. For this reason, men with prostate cancer often develop osteopenia or osteoporosis in the rest of their skeleton. In advanced prostate cancer, the flow of calcium into the involved bone sites can be so great that patients suffer from an abnormally low blood calcium level. The body responds to this challenge by producing parathyroid hormone, a hormone that breaks down bone to liberate enough calcium to restore normal blood levels of this mineral. Not only does this process accelerate the destruction of the bone not involved in the cancer, but also it causes bone pain.

Calcitriol is a very effective treatment for an elevated parathyroid hormone level and can significantly slow bone breakdown as well as lessen the generalized bone discomfort.

For all of these reasons, I don't think that there is any controversy about the fact that it is important for prostate cancer patients to maintain an adequate calcitriol blood level. The major controversy is how best to do this.

Calcitriol & Prostate Cancer

Until recently, the published clinical studies on prostate cancer have focused on how best to administer calcitriol in order to obtain an optimal benefit. However, administering calcitriol causes the body to produce more of a protein that can destroy it: the 24-hydroxylase. This has led to several proposals of how to protect calcitriol once it is in the bloodstream. Drs. Peehl and Feldman from Stanford University proposed one interesting idea. These authors noted that ketoconazole, a drug used to treat fungal infections, blocked 24-hydroxylase's ability to destroy calcitriol. While ketoconazole is used at doses as high as 400 mg every eight hours as a treatment for prostate cancer, a dose as low as 200 mg a day may be enough to block the protein involved in destroying calcitriol.

Another approach that has been proposed is to administer calcitriol with vitamin D or calcidiol; the idea is to overwhelm the 24-hydroxylase. In our clinic, for years we've treated patients with calcitriol at a dose of 0.5 mcgs a day. In a vast majority of men this dose is sufficient to keep their calcitriol blood levels above the 40 pg/ml threshold. When we increased the dose of calcitriol to 0.75 or 1 mcg daily, patients would commonly develop elevated blood calcium levels—a sure indication of too much calcitriol. In fact, multiple clinical trials show that a major limitation in using calcitriol to treat cancer is that it dangerously elevates blood calcium. I regard this as proof positive that for many patients there is no problem delivering as much calcitriol as the patient can tolerate. Another, much more interesting approach was recently tested by Reinhold Vieth, the author of the 1999 paper that stimulated many of us to reevaluate the optimal daily vitamin D dose. Vieth treated fifteen patients who had relapsed following surgery or radiation therapy with 2,000 IU of vitamin D (cholecalciferol) a day. Remember, this is the amount most people need for general good health. In nine patients (60%), their PSA either declined or stayed the same for as long as twenty-one months. The median PSA doubling time, an indicator of the rate of cancer growth, went from 14.3 months before vitamin D to 25 months after.

This approach has several advantages over calcitriol administration. Vitamin D is widely available over the counter while calcitriol requires a prescription. Vitamin D is very cheap while calcitriol is quite expensive: a problem if your insurance does not cover prescription drugs. Vitamin D and its major metabolite, calcidiol, disappear slowly from the body, while calcitriol is cleared quite rapidly. As a result, if you miss several days of vitamin D there is much less of an impact than there is with calcitriol. There are some potential limitations to vitamin D, but these should be easy to handle. If you ingest a lot of calcium and/or phosphate (such as that in diet colas or milk), the formation of calcitriol from vitamin D and calcidiol will decrease dramatically. If you eat a lot of sugar, especially fruit sugar (fructose), you may suddenly form too much calcitriol, leading to dangerously high calcium levels.

Also, the calcitriol that appears in the blood following vitamin D administration is largely formed in the kidneys. Many men with prostate cancer have damaged kidneys. They may have had the flow of urine blocked by the cancer long enough that their kidneys are no longer functioning well. A catheter may have caused bacterial infections of the bladder and kidney. Zometa, one of the drugs commonly used to treat advanced prostate cancer, can cause kidney damage. A more subtle form of kidney damage also develops as we age. On average, an 80 year-old has half the kidney function of a 20 year-old. As a result, men over 80 may not form calcitriol nearly as well as younger patients. In patients who do not make sufficient calcitriol when they are taking these higher doses of vitamin D3, oral calcitriol is a reasonable alternative. As an added advantage, if your physician demonstrates the combination of impaired kidney function, low calcitriol blood levels and an elevated parathyroid hormone level, it should be easier to get your insurance to cover the cost of the calcitriol.

What About Sunbathing?

Even ten to twenty minutes of summer sun exposure can produce greater than 10,000 IU of vitamin D. Furthermore, excess vitamin D made during the summer can be stored in the body fat deposits for use during the winter months. It would seem a simple matter to just make sure that you get sufficient exposure to the summer sun. This simple idea has become a hotly contested issue. Several books, such as *The UV Advantage* by Michael Holick, have tried to make a very strong case for this approach. Dermatologists, on the other hand, point out that sun exposure causes premature aging of the skin and increases the risk of skin cancers of various sorts. My own take on this issue is that sun exposure is a fine way to get vitamin D3 in large amounts, but sun exposure has several problems. Chronic sun exposure does indeed speed skin aging. It also plays a major role in cataract development. Of even greater concern, sun exposure suppresses immune system function. In one recent paper in Nature Medicine, investigators show that sun-induced immunosuppression was strong enough to protect organ grafts from rejection! This is the last thing a cancer patient needs. In all fairness, I would point out that all of these problems are much more severe for those without pigment in their skin. Perhaps the fact that I'm fair-skinned biases my view of this controversy. Nevertheless, vitamin D3 is readily available in pill form and inexpensive as well. Oral vitamin D3 does not cause skin aging, skin cancer, cataracts, or major immunosuppression. For this reason, I strongly favor oral vitamin D3 as compared with sun exposure.

If you have dark skin, especially if you are African American, sun exposure may be a more attractive alternative. Darker skin is less likely to be damaged by moderate sun exposure. Also, at least one study suggests that sun is much less likely to cause significant immuno-suppression in African Americans. However, you do need to be aware that it takes much more sun exposure to lead to similar levels of vitamin D3 production and this may be difficult to fit into a busy life. In fact, it can take ten times longer for an African American to make the same amount of vitamin D as it takes a blond or red haired individual. In the end, oral vitamin D3 may still be the most practical approach.

My Recommendation

As I mentioned before, for most men with prostate cancer and as well as those interested in preventing the disease, I recommend taking 4000 IU vitamin D daily although the commonly recommended daily allowance for Vitamin D is only 400 IU. I routinely measure the PSA every 3 months in men with prostate cancer and try to attain a serum calcidiol or 25-hydroxyvitamin D level of 50-80 nmol/L. At least initially, I would also measure the calcidiol and calcitriol blood levels with the same frequency. If it proved impossible to keep calcitriol blood levels above 40 pg/ml, I would consider switching to calcitriol.

Men with kidney damage or over 80 years old may very likely require calcitriol rather than vitamin D. The starting dose is 0.5 mcgs per day. Again, we'd measure parathyroid hormone levels and adjust the dose to normalize the parathyroid hormone level.

If you make it a practice to avoid the sun, then you may need as much as 5,000 IU. The majority of Americans don't get close to this amount of vitamin

D per day, and as a result, vitamin D deficiency is common here. Vitamin D deficiency exacerbates many common diseases.

We live in an age when obesity and the diabetes that commonly follows are increasing at stunning rates. Vitamin D deficiency exacerbates both. Lack of adequate vitamin D also increases the risk of hypertension. In turn, high blood pressure, diabetes, and obesity foster the development of heart disease; inadequate vitamin D levels increase the risk of heart attacks and congestive heart failure.

Falls are common in the elderly and are major factors leading to hospitalizations, nursing home placements, and subsequent death. Several clinical trials show vitamin D supplements markedly reduce the risk of falling. Many of the elderly who experience such falls also have osteoporosis, which increases the likelihood that they'll fracture bones when they fall, further complicating recovery. So making sure you have enough vitamin D reduces your risk of osteoporosis and fracture.

Now, the four leading causes of cancer death are lung, colon, breast, and prostate. Vitamin D reduces death risk from all four of these.

Lycopene

Lycopene is a cartenoid and a powerful antioxidant. Unlike other orange-pigmented cartenoids, such as beta carotene, lycopene is colored red. Tomatoes, red watermelon, and pink grapefruit are the three richest sources of lycopene and owe their red color to this pigment. Of the carotenoids, lycopene is also the most effective antioxidant.

There are a range of papers that demonstrate lycopene's effect on slowing the growth of metastatic prostate cancer. Increased blood and prostate lycopene levels are associated with a rapid impact on prostate cancer, limiting the extent of the disease at the time of surgery and significantly enhancing the effectiveness of hormonal therapy. The three most recent studies are, to my mind, the most significant because they are randomized controlled trials.

The first, by Kucuk et al., randomized twenty-six men to placebo or to lycopene 30 mg a day for three weeks before radical prostatectomy. At the time of surgery, the patients who received lycopene, compared with patients taking the placebo, had smaller tumors, less involvement of surgical margins and/or extra-prostatic tissues with cancer and less diffuse involvement of the prostate by high grade prostatic intraepithelial neoplasia. Their PSAs were also lower.

In the second study, Ansari, et al. randomized 54 patients with metastatic prostate cancer to surgical castration alone or surgical castration plus 2 mg twice a day of lycopene. The lycopene dosage was relatively low—a mere 2 mg twice a day.

Over a two-year time period, the patients who received lycopene after castration did much better than those who did not: their results suggested that a very modest dose of lycopene can significantly enhance hormonal therapy's ability to control metastatic prostate cancer.

In the third clinical trial, Bowen, et al. randomized patients to a placebo group or a tomato sauce group (which contained enough lycopene to deliver 30 mg a day) for three weeks before radical prostatectomy. Bowen found that mean serum PSA levels decreased by 17.5% as a result of lycopene treatment. The number of dying cancer cells was also greater in the samples from patients treated with lycopene.

And, not surprisingly, given what we now know about the Mediterranean diet, lycopene and other carotenoids appear to have a significant impact on many factors associated with developing type II diabetes mellitus, a common problem here in America. Ylonen, et al. found that in men, dietary carotenoids (including lycopene) were inversely associated with fasting blood glucose concentrations as well as with insulin resistance.

A Lycopene-rich Diet

A diet high in tomato products and thus lycopene is associated with a reduced risk of prostate cancer. The greatest protection was associated with an intake of 10 or more servings of tomato products each week. In the tomato, lycopene is contained within small packets that are not readily broken down by the stomach and intestines. Cooking tomatoes significantly improves the ease with which you can absorb lycopene and is associated with the greatest impact on the risk of prostate cancer. Many holistic practitioners advocate the use of only raw fruits and vegetables. While this might be true in some cases, it seems appropriate to make clear that the foods that we consume are complex agents with very specific chemical components that need to be evaluated individually. In other words, lumping all the fruits and vegetables into one category in terms of preparation may not be the best idea. In terms of diet and lifestyle, too many people ascribe to a philosophy without evaluating it with the thoroughness required. We want our readers to know that it is important to take the time to understand everything that they put into their body and why. In the case of tomatoes as well as other foods, such as broccoli, cooking is required for the human gastrointestinal tract to optimally process the vegetables.

The simplest approach to maximixe lycopene intake is to have an eight-ounce glass of tomato or V8 juice every morning with breakfast. For dinner, spaghetti, vegetarian chili or other tomato-based dishes can be used. With this diet, it is easy to eat at least 10 servings of tomatoes a week, a more pleasurable and less expensive way than taking lycopene capsules.

Why You Should Take The Supplement Anyway

Cooked whole tomatoes, or tomato sauces, have a wide range of chemicals other than lycopene that possibly have a positive impact on health and I encourage you to incorporate them into your diet. But I have to point out that most of the human clinical trials with lycopene have used tomato oleoresin in pill form. So I recommend you take the 10 mg supplement with each meal and eat a diet rich in lycopene.

You Can't Overdose

In the last fifteen years I haven't found a single report of any side effects attributed to lycopene.

Of course, we also know that lycopene, once in the body, persists for several days. If you start to take lycopene, your blood and tissue levels will steadily increase each day for one week. This means missing a day or so may have only a modest impact on the concentration of lycopene in your tissues.

Why Three 10mg Doses and Not One 30 mg Dose?

There appears to be no advantage to single doses greater than 10 mg. There's roughly 10 mg of lycopene in one teaspoon of tomato paste. If you're interested in pushing lycopene to the limit, you'd probably be better served by taking 10 mg or less of lycopene, as pills or tomato products, several times a day.

Diwadkar-Navsariwala, et al. reported detailed information on the absorption of lycopene after various oral doses, which ranged from 10 to 120 mg. No matter how much lycopene they took at any given time, 80% of the subjects in this study absorbed less than 6 mg of lycopene after a single oral dose. This suggests that there is a maximum amount of lycopene that you can absorb and that there's no real advantage to taking very large doses at one time. So you may be better off taking multiple, small doses (less than 10 mg) several times a day. Of course, this idea hasn't been tested clinically.

Vitamin E

Vitamin E is a powerful antioxidant that has been tested as a treatment against a range of diseases, including prostate cancer. Most prostate cancer patients take vitamin E, and I recommend it to my patients as a means of slowing prostate cancer growth.

There's actually a variety of laboratory and clinical evidence supporting vitamin E use in prostate cancer. In the lab, testosterone exposure causes oxidative damage to prostate cells. Vitamin E and selenium lessen that oxidative damage. In human prostate specimens, oxidative damage to the genetic material in this tissue appears with the onset of puberty and increases with each decade. There is a tight correlation between the amount of oxidative damage and the incidence of prostate cancer in these prostate specimens. Vitamin E not only acts as an antioxidant but also triggers apoptosis (suicide) in prostate cancer cells. Because of this, the pharmaceutical industry has developed synthetic chemical analogs of vitamin E that, in the lab, kill prostate cancer. These analogs are in initial clinical trials. As we said earlier, among the forms of vitamin E, gamma- and delta-tocopherol appear much more active than alpha-tocopherol. The incidence of prostate cancer is lower among men with higher gamma-tocopherol levels.

The key randomized controlled trial on vitamin E and prostate cancer is the "Alpha-Tocopherol, Beta-Carotene Cancer Prevention Study." This clinical trial divided 29,133 men into four groups: one group took no supplements; one took only alpha-tocopherol; another took only beta-carotene, and the fourth group took both alpha-tocopherol and beta-carotene. The men who took alpha-tocopherol alone had a 40% reduction in prostate cancer death. Keep in mind that the dose of alpha-tocopherol was only 50 IU. Furthermore, the alpha-tocopherol used was synthetic and thus had only half the activity of the natural form.

In light of more recent information, it would have been interesting to see what might have happened if gamma- or delta-tocopherol had been used. Also, we have no clinical trial information on higher doses. These results are now being further tested and refined in the SELECT trial that looks at selenium, alpha-tocopherol and their combination in a well-designed randomized controlled trial.

Again, the dose of vitamin E used in this study was actually quite low—50 IUs a day. A low dose is very safe and costs only about 10 cents a day. This is important because, as those of you who followed the Vitamin E scare last fall know, there's a significant bleeding risk if you take vitamin E in higher doses. (Until we have more information about the potential bleeding risks of high dose Vitamin E, I'm now recommending you take vitamin E in doses at or below 200 mg of gamma tocopherol per day.) This is also why you should be careful about taking high dose vitamin E in combination with other agents, such as coumadin, that decrease blood clotting and why your surgeon may ask you to stop taking vitamin E before a major surgery.

Selenium

Selenium is a critical part of the enzyme glutathione peroxidase, which converts hydrogen peroxide to water using glutathione. In glutathione peroxidase, selenium is linked to cysteine in the form of selenocysteine. There is growing evidence that selenium also plays an important role in a range of other, less well-understood, selenium-containing antioxidant proteins. Severe selenium deficiency is associated with sudden death from heart failure.

Moderate selenium deficiency is associated with an increased risk of cancer and various infectious diseases, such as pneumonia. The most widely available form, and the one that has been used in most of the clinical trials, is selenium-yeast. Selenomethionine is also available but less well understood in humans. Some vendors market selenocysteine, which is probably quite active because it is the form found in glutathione peroxidase. In addition to its capacity to enhance the destruction of hydrogen peroxide, selenium has been shown to kill prostate cancer cells directly. And in the laboratory, selenium appears to enhance the capacity of chemotherapy agents, including Taxol and Adriamycin. I suggest you take 200 mcgs a day.

Your Genes May Determine the Value of Lycopene, Selenium & Vitamin E

As we just discussed, these three supplements are antioxidants and so you should expect that their value would be determined by the severity of oxidative damage in the prostate gland. There are several proteins that help lessen the amount of oxidative damage in the tissues in your body. These proteins act by destroying the oxidants that cause this damage. For example, hydrogen peroxide is capable of causing severe oxidative damage and two proteins are responsible for eliminating this dangerous compound: catalase and glutathione peroxidase. The latter depends on selenium for its activity and thus the elimination of hydrogen peroxide is more effective if you have enough selenium in your diet. Superoxide is another dangerous oxidant and the protein, superoxide dismutase, speeds the elimination of superoxide. One form of superoxide dismutase that contains manganese appears to be particularly important. Two forms of this enzyme have been described in humans: one that is very active and one that is not. Those with the less active form of this enzyme seem to be at increased risk for the development of prostate cancer as well as aging in general. Vitamin E, selenium and lycopene appear to be much more active in reducing the risk of prostate cancer in those with the less active form of this protein. This is just what you would expect. Less active superoxide dismuatase means more oxidative damage and thus a greater chance of benefiting from antioxidants like vitamin E, selenium, and lycopene. For those with the less active form of superoxide dismutase, the highest level of selenium was associated with an 80% drop in the risk of aggressive prostate cancer. In contrast, those with the more active form of superoxide dismutase experienced only a 30% decline. When lycopene, vitamin E and selenium were combined, the men with the inactive form of superoxide dismutase had greater than a ten fold decline in the risk of aggressive prostate cancer!

Unfortunately, you can't run out and have your manganese superoxide dismutase protein tested to see if you have the active or inactive form: it is still a research tool.

Omega 3s

Studies show that the more fish you eat, the lower your risk of developing a variety of cancers. In the case of prostate cancer, the most detailed population study was done by Augustsson, et al., which followed more than 47,000 men for twelve years. While fish consumption tended to reduce the overall prostate cancer risk, the most dramatic impact was on the risk of developing metastases. For each 500 mg increase in daily fish oil consumption, there was a 24% reduction in risk of metastatic prostate cancer.

With regard to prostate cancer, the issue is a bit more complicated because detailed information is only available for fish consumption, not fish oil capsules. My best guess is that 4-6,000 mg a day would be sufficient to give you most of the benefits.

You may ask: how much fish oil can someone take safely? Are there any serious side effects from high doses? One side effect I've found is fish oil's propensity to reduce the tendency for people to develop clots in their arteries. Questions then arise: what about the impact on normal clotting? Does fish oil increase the risk of bleeding? While I have repeatedly heard these concerns expressed, I can find no evidence to support this worry. Some also claim that it's not safe to combine fish oil with drugs that alter blood clotting, such as aspirin or coumadin. Again, I can find no evidence to support this claim.

There are other benefits to consuming fish or fish oil. There is some indication that fish oil can lessen weight loss associated with advanced cancer. One clinical trial gave increasing amounts of fish oil to patients with advanced cancer who were losing weight. They found that these patients could consume up to twenty-one 1,000 mg capsules with minimal problems. The complaints were limited to some gastric distress from the large amount of fat and of a "fishy" odor. Based on my experience, the only way advanced cancer patients would be able to take twenty-one 1,000 mg capsules is if the oil was a very high quality product.

Fresh fish and fish oil capsules spoil quickly if not handled properly. Fish fat readily turns rancid. A strong "fishy" smell represents a sure sign of rancid or spoiled fish fat. Lack of a strong "fishy" odor is an excellent sign of quality fish and fish oil. Needless to say, you should avoid any supplements with this odor. This is a serious problem with many cheap brands of fish oil capsules, and I've spent considerable time hunting for quality brands. To obtain good fish oil, you need to process the fish while it's fresh and protect the oil from heat and light. You also need to fortify the fish oil with antioxidants to prevent it from turning rancid. Oil from even the best vendor can turn rancid if it's stored or shipped inappropriately. It's important that the oil be kept in a cool, dark place. Once opened, store your bottle in the refrigerator or freezer. While I cannot claim to have tested every product on the market, there are several that appear to be consistently high quality: Nordic Naturals, Life Extension Foundation, and Barry Sears OmegaRx brands. I think you will find these products worth the extra cost.

What If You're A Vegetarian Or Vegan?

You face a unique problem: common plant sources of omega 3 fats are rich in ALA, but lack DHA and EPA. But humans—especially men—do a very poor job of converting ALA to EPA and DHA. So strict vegans and vegetarians risk developing serious omega 3 deficiencies.

Others are reluctant to eat fish because of possible environmental contaminants like mercury, dioxin, or PCBs, and have asked if there's a plant-based alternative to fish oil. Fish don't make their own EPA and DHA, but obtain DHA from algae. It stands to reason, then, that we too can obtain our DHA from algae.

In fact, Martek Pharmaceuticals has patented a process of growing a DHA-producing microalgae (crypthecodinium cohnii) and extracting the omega 3 fatty acid. Much of the DHA Martek produces is used in infant feeding formulas as well as in animal feed, but it's also available in 100 and 200 mg capsules under the trade name Neuromins®. If you want to use plant sources of omega 3 fats, Neuromins represents a much higher quality product than flax seed oil or any other plant-based omega 3 fat source.

Soy Isoflavones

We now have our first clinical trial showing that soy isoflavones have a major impact on human prostate cancer progression. Hussain, et al. administered soy isoflavones (100 mg twice a day) to men with prostate cancer. Among men whose cancer recurred after surgery or radiation therapy, soy isoflavone administration slowed cancer growth in 84% of cases. Even in men who had hormone-refractory prostate cancer, soy slowed cancer growth in 35% of patients. The brand of soy isoflavone used in this study was Novasoy (www.novasoy.com). This is a product of Archer Daniels Midland, one of the largest agricultural companies. However, I have no reason to suspect that the benefits were unique to the Novasoy product.

In fact, it may well be that any of a number of commercial soy isoflavone concentrates would do just as well. Dose does seem to be important. Another study that used 80 mg (as opposed to 200 mg) as a daily total dose failed to demonstrate any advantage to soy isoflavones. These studies have failed to document the stimulation of prostate cancer that Dr. Leibowitz has reported, suggesting that this is a relatively rare phenomenon. In fact, soy appears to be beneficial for a vast majority of men whose cancers recur after surgery and radiation therapy. I must say that part of the reason the trial by Dr. Hussain impresses me is that she is an accomplished medical oncologist who is one of the lead clinical investigators involved in the development of chemotherapy for prostate cancer. Since 2000, she authored or coauthored well over 20 papers on prostate cancer.

But it is important to point out that there are major questions that are not yet answered. I would like to see Dr. Hussain's observation confirmed.

Further, it would be best if soy isoflavones were subjected to a randomized controlled trial so we could determine if adding soy actually prolongs a patient's life or delays the need for either hormonal therapy or chemotherapy. Finally, a large randomized controlled trial would allow us to more accurately determine if there really are a significant number of men who experience increased prostate cancer growth after adding soy isoflavones to their diet. Despite these issues, I have made soy a major part of my diet and am taking 100 mg of soy isoflavones twice a day. Nevertheless, I strongly suggest you carefully monitor your PSA and any other evidence of cancer progression on the outside chance that you may be one of the few men with a cancer that can be stimulated by soy. Also, if you have a family history of dementia or are seeing a physician for this problem, I suggest you carefully review the pros and cons of soy use with your doctor prior to adding it to your program.

You can also boost your soy intake by eating endamame, tofu, soy milk, or a soy shake product like Revival Soy. All are available at most grocery stores by now, or, of course, via the web.

Final Thoughts...

Now that you have learned the theory behind the complex art of effecting curative treatment for prostate cancer, it's time to put the theory into practice. After reading this book patients and their loved ones should be well equipped with all the tools available for crafting the best treatment strategy for their specific cases. We encourage patients to take this guidebook with them to their doctors and start using these tools as soon as possible.

We also encourage you to pass the information this book has to offer to your support group, your friends, and, in regards to the dietary information, to your sons.

Unfortunately, so many men and medical professionals still remain unaware of the treatment advances in hormonal therapy and how these advances can be used either alone or in combination with "traditional" treatments. For decades prostate cancer has been treated as an "old man's disease" and therefore a "lesser" disease by the powers that govern medical research and treatment. Yet, in my practice I am seeing more men under fifty-years old than ever before. The good news is that both the research and my clinical experience suggest that there are also more options for treatment success than ever before.

I'd like to stress how important it is to choose a positive and open-minded health team who is willing to work with you to not only treat your cancer but also to prolong your survival and quality of life. I use the term "team" to emphasize your participation in this endeavor. By learning the proverbial game and all of the strategies that have worked for the "pros" we sincerely hope that you will become active in 1) educating yourself and your physicians about the latest treatment options and 2) choosing the right diet and supplementation regimen to compliment whatever treatment modality you decide is best for your specific stage in the game

With any life-threatening illness it's easy to despair, especially when confronted with a throng of medical professionals who are actually trained in medical school to detach from their patients for their own emotional self-interest. While this practice might enhance a certain diagnostic objectivity, it astounds me how many physicians take this to the extreme level of callousness when a positive bedside manner is crucial to both the emotional and, as we illustrated earlier in this book, the physiological well being of the patients under their care.

The underlying need for this book was hinged on hope: my hope as it pertained to my own disease treatment and bringing that hope to other men like me who have been told their situations are dire enough to put a cap on their life expectancy. While I was 55 at the age of my diagnosis the prospect of living five or ten more years did not appeal to me, as you might imagine. My treatment was based on defying the current expectations of the prostate cancer industry and with an undetectable PSA after seven years I believe I've been successful.

My final hope is that the information in this book will be as useful to you as it was to me, as I understand that most men facing a prostate cancer diagnosis are not in fact medical oncologists with thirty years of experience to help them with their treatment choice. With that said, this book can be considered a flashlight for all the men who were and are more in the dark than I was after my diagnosis.

With any luck it may light the way to a safer and happier place.

Appendix

References

References

Chapters 1 &2

1. Leibowitz, R.L. and S.J. Tucker, Treatment of localized prostate cancer with intermittent triple androgen blockade: preliminary results in 110 consecutive patients. Oncologist, 2001. 6(2): p. 177-82.

Chapter 3

2. Deguchi, T., et al., Detection of micrometastatic prostate cancer cells in lymph nodes by reverse transcriptase-polymerase chain reaction. Cancer Res, 1993. 53(22): p. 5350-4.

3. Deguchi, T., et al., Detection of micrometastatic prostate cancer cells in the bone marrow of patients with prostate cancer. Br J Cancer, 1997. 75(5): p. 634-8.

4. Ellis, W.J., et al., Detection and isolation of prostate cancer cells from peripheral blood and bone marrow. Urology, 2003. 61(2): p. 277-81.

5. Fadlon, E.J., et al., Detection of circulating prostate-specific antigen-positive cells in patients with prostate cancer by flow cytometry and reverse transcription polymerase chain reaction. Br J Cancer, 1996. 74(3): p. 400-5.

6. Mansi, J.L., et al., Detection of tumor cells in bone marrow of patients with prostatic carcinoma by immunocytochemical techniques. J Urol, 1988. 139(3): p. 545-8.

7. Martinez-Pineiro, L., et al., Molecular staging of prostatic cancer with RT-PCR assay for prostate-specific antigen in peripheral blood and lymph nodes: comparison with standard histological staging and immunohistochemical assessment of occult regional lymph node metastases. Eur Urol, 2003. 43(4): p. 342-50.

8. Shariat, S.F., et al., Comparison of immunohistochemistry with reverse transcription-PCR for the detection of micrometastatic prostate cancer in lymph nodes. Cancer Res, 2003. 63(15): p. 4662-70.

9. Wood, D.P., Jr., et al., Identification of bone marrow micrometastases in patients with prostate cancer. Cancer, 1994. 74(9): p. 2533-40.

10. Wood, D.P., Jr., et al., Sensitivity of immunohistochemistry and polymerase chain reaction in detecting prostate cancer cells in bone marrow. J Histochem Cytochem, 1994. 42(4): p. 505-11.

11. Borley, N., et al., Laparoscopic pelvic lymph node dissection allows significantly more accurate staging in "high-risk" prostate cancer compared to MRI or CT. Scand J Urol Nephrol, 2003. 37(5): p. 382-6.

12. Brossner, C., et al., Lymphatic drainage of prostatic transition and peripheral zones visualized on a three-dimensional workstation. Urology, 2001. 57(2): p. 389-93.

13. Cellini, N., et al., Lymphatic drainage and CTV in carcinoma of the prostate. Rays, 2003. 28(3): p. 337-41.

14. Cheng, L., et al., Cancer volume of lymph node metastasis predicts progression in prostate cancer. Am J Surg Pathol, 1998. 22(12): p. 1491-500.

15. Cheng, L., et al., Risk of prostate carcinoma death in patients with lymph node metastasis. Cancer, 2001. 91(1): p. 66-73.

16. Daneshmand, S., et al., Prognosis of patients with lymph node positive prostate cancer following radical prostatectomy: long-term results. J Urol, 2004. 172(6 Pt 1): p. 2252-5.

17. Deguchi, T., et al., Detection of micrometastatic prostate cancer cells in lymph nodes by reverse transcriptase-polymerase chain reaction. Cancer Res, 1993. 53(22): p. 5350-4.
18. Deguchi, T., et al., Prostate cancer micrometastases to lymph nodes. Urology, 1997. 50(5): p. 826-7.

19. Edelstein, R.A., et al., Implications of prostate micrometastases in pelvic lymph nodes: an archival tissue study. Urology, 1996. 47(3): p. 370-5.

20. Hering, F., et al., Does microinvasion of the capsule and/or micrometastases in regional lymph nodes influence disease-free survival after radical prostatectomy? Br J Urol, 1990. 66(2): p. 177-81.

21. Kothari, P.S., et al., Incidence, location, and significance of periprostatic and periseminal vesicle lymph nodes in prostate cancer. Am J Surg Pathol, 2001. 25(11): p. 1429-32.

22. McLaughlin, A.P., et al., Prostatic carcinoma: incidence and location of unsuspected lymphatic metastases. J Urol, 1976. 115(1): p. 89-94.

23. McNeal, J.E., Prostatic microcarcinomas in relation to cancer origin and the evolution to clinical cancer. Cancer, 1993. 71(3 Suppl): p. 984-91.

24. Oyan, B., H. Engin, and S. Yalcin, Generalized lymphadenopathy: a rare presentation of disseminated prostate cancer. Med Oncol, 2002. 19(3): p. 177-9.

25. Palapattu, G.S., et al., Prostate specific antigen progression in men with lymph node metastases following radical prostatectomy: results of long-term followup. J Urol, 2004. 172(5 Pt 1): p. 1860-4.

26. Raboy, A., H. Adler, and P. Albert, Extraperitoneal endoscopic pelvic lymph node dissection: a review of 125 patients. J Urol, 1997. 158(6): p. 2202-4; discussion 2204-5.

27. Schmid, H.P., et al., Impact of minimal lymph node metastasis on long-term prognosis after radical prostatectomy. Eur Urol, 1997. 31(1): p. 11-6.

28. Smith, J.A., Jr. and R.G. Middleton, Implications of volume of nodal metastasis in patients with adenocarcinoma of the prostate. J Urol, 1985. 133(4): p. 617-9.

29. Spencer, J.A. and S.J. Golding, Patterns of lymphatic metastases at recurrence of prostate cancer: CT findings. Clin Radiol, 1994. 49(6): p. 404-7.

30. Steinberg, G.D., et al., Management of stage D1 adenocarcinoma of the prostate: the Johns Hopkins experience 1974 to 1987. J Urol, 1990. 144(6): p. 1425-32.

31. Wawroschek, F., et al., Radioisotope guided pelvic lymph node dissection for prostate cancer. J Urol, 2001. 166(5): p. 1715-9.

32. Wawroschek, F., et al., The sentinel lymph node concept in prostate cancer - first results of gamma probe-guided sentinel lymph node identification. Eur Urol, 1999. 36(6): p. 595-600.

33. Zincke, H. and D.C. Utz, Observations on surgical management of carcinoma of prostate with limited nodal metastases. Urology, 1984. 24(2): p. 137-45.

34. Zwergel, U., et al., Lymph node positive prostate cancer: long-term survival data after radical prostatectomy. J Urol, 2004. 171(3): p. 1128-31.

35. DeWyngaert, J.K., et al., Procedure for unmasking localization information from ProstaScint scans for prostate radiation therapy treatment planning. Int J Radiat Oncol Biol Phys, 2004. 60(2): p. 654-62.

36. Harisinghani, M.G., et al., Noninvasive detection of clinically occult lymph-node metastases in prostate cancer. N Engl J Med, 2003. 348(25): p. 2491-9.

37. Sodee, D.B., et al., The prognostic significance of indium-111-capromab penetide. J Clin Oncol, 2004. 22(2): p. 379-80; author reply 380-1.

Chapters 4, 5 & 6

38. Culig, Z., et al., Switch from antagonist to agonist of the androgen receptor bicalutamide is associated with prostate tumour progression in a new model system. Br J Cancer, 1999. 81(2): p. 242-51.

39. Gregory, C.W., et al., Androgen receptor stabilization in recurrent prostate cancer is associated with hypersensitivity to low androgen. Cancer Res, 2001. 61(7): p. 2892-8.

40. Leibowitz, R.L. and S.J. Tucker, Treatment of localized prostate cancer with intermittent triple androgen blockade: preliminary results in 110 consecutive patients. Oncologist, 2001. 6(2): p. 177-82.

41. Brown, R.S., et al., Amplification of the androgen receptor gene in bone metastases from hormone-refractory prostate cancer. J Pathol, 2002. 198(2): p. 237-44.

42. Dockery, F., et al., Testosterone suppression in men with prostate cancer leads to an increase in arterial stiffness and hyperinsulinaemia. Clin Sci (Lond), 2003. 104(2): p. 195-201

43. Higano, C.S., Side effects of androgen deprivation therapy: monitoring and minimizing toxicity. Urology, 2003. 61(2 Suppl 1): p. 32-8.

44. Holzbeierlein, J.M., E. Castle, and J.B. Thrasher, Complications of androgen deprivation therapy: prevention and treatment. Oncology (Huntingt), 2004. 18(3): p. 303-9; discussion 310, 315, 319-21.

45. de Leval, J., et al., Intermittent versus continuous total androgen blockade in the treatment of patients with advanced hormone-naive prostate cancer: results of a prospective randomized multicenter trial. Clin Prostate Cancer, 2002. 1(3): p. 163-71.

46. Pether, M., et al., Intermittent androgen suppression in prostate cancer: an update of the Vancouver experience. Can J Urol, 2003. 10(2): p. 1809-14.

47. Xu, T., et al., Effect of surgical castration on risk factors for arteriosclerosis of patients with prostate cancer. Chin Med J (Engl), 2002. 115(9): p. 1336-40.

Chapter 7

48. Han, M., et al., An evaluation of the decreasing incidence of positive surgical margins in a large retropubic prostatectomy series. J Urol, 2004. 171(1): p. 23-6.

49. Khan, M.A., et al., Long-term cancer control of radical prostatectomy in men younger than 50 years of age: update 2003. Urology, 2003. 62(1): p. 86-91; discussion 91-2.

50. Han, M., et al., Biochemical (prostate specific antigen) recurrence probability following radical prostatectomy for clinically localized prostate cancer. J Urol, 2003. 169(2): p. 517-23.

51. Carter, H.B., et al., Expectant management of nonpalpable prostate cancer with curative intent: preliminary results. J Urol, 2002. 167(3): p. 1231-4.

52. Carter, H.B., et al., Expectant management of prostate cancer with curative intent. Eur Urol, 2001. 39 Suppl 4: p. 24.

53. Pilepich, M.V., et al., Phase III trial of androgen suppression using goserelin in unfavorable- prognosis carcinoma of the prostate treated with definitive radiotherapy: report of Radiation Therapy Oncology Group Protocol 85-31. J Clin Oncol, 1997. 15(3): p. 1013-21.

54. Bolla, M., et al., Improved survival in patients with locally advanced prostate cancer treated with radiotherapy and goserelin. N Engl J Med, 1997. 337(5): p. 295-300.

55. Cheng, L., et al., Cancer volume of lymph node metastasis predicts progression in prostate cancer. Am J Surg Pathol, 1998. 22(12): p. 1491-500.

56. Cheng, L., et al., p53 alteration in regional lymph node metastases from prostate carcinoma: a marker for progression? Cancer, 1999. 85(11): p. 2455-9.

57. Cheng, L., et al., Cell proliferation in prostate cancer patients with lymph node metastasis: a marker for progression. Clin Cancer Res, 1999. 5(10): p. 2820-3.

58. Cheng, L., et al., Risk of prostate carcinoma death in patients with lymph node metastasis. Cancer, 2001. 91(1): p. 66-73.

59. Ghavamian, R., et al., Radical retropubic prostatectomy plus orchiectomy versus orchiectomy alone for pTxN+ prostate cancer: a matched comparison. J Urol, 1999. 161(4): p. 1223-7; discussion 1227-8.

60. Messing, E.M., et al., Immediate hormonal therapy compared with observation after radical prostatectomy and pelvic lymphadenectomy in men with node-positive prostate cancer. N Engl J Med, 1999. 341(24): p. 1781-8.

61. Seay, T.M., M.L. Blute, and H. Zincke, Long-term outcome in patients with pTxN+ adenocarcinoma of prostate treated with radical prostatectomy and early androgen ablation. J Urol, 1998. 159(2): p. 357-64.

62. Ward, J.F. and H. Zincke, Radical prostatectomy for the patient with locally advanced prostate cancer. Curr Urol Rep, 2003. 4(3): p. 196-204.

63. Zagars, G.K., et al., Early androgen ablation for stage D1 (N1 to N3, M0) prostate cancer: prognostic variables and outcome. J Urol, 1994. 151(5): p. 1330-3.

64. Bolla, M., et al., Improved survival in patients with locally advanced prostate cancer treated with radiotherapy and goserelin. N Engl J Med, 1997. 337(5): p. 295-300.

65. Bolla, M., Adjuvant Hormonal Treatment with Radiotherapy for Locally Advanced Prostate Cancer. Eur Urol, 1998. 35 Suppl S1: p. 23-26.

66. Bolla, M., Adjuvant hormonal treatment with radiotherapy for locally advanced prostate cancer. Eur Urol, 1999. 35 Suppl 1: p. 23-5; discussion 26.

67. Roach, M., 3rd, et al., Predicting long-term survival, and the need for hormonal therapy: a meta-analysis of RTOG prostate cancer trials. Int J Radiat Oncol Biol Phys, 2000. 47(3): p. 617-27.

68. Horwitz, E.M., et al., Subset analysis of RTOG 85-31 and 86-10 indicates an advantage for long-term vs. short-term adjuvant hormones for patients with locally advanced non-metastatic prostate cancer treated with radiation therapy. Int J Radiat Oncol Biol Phys, 2001. 49(4): p. 947-56.

69. Lawton, C.A., et al., Updated results of the phase III Radiation Therapy Oncology Group (RTOG) trial 85-31 evaluating the potential benefit of androgen suppression following standard radiation therapy for unfavorable prognosis carcinoma of the prostate. Int J Radiat Oncol Biol Phys, 2001. 49(4): p. 937-46.

70. Pilepich, M.V., et al., Phase III radiation therapy oncology group (RTOG) trial 86-10 of androgen deprivation adjuvant to definitive radiotherapy in locally advanced carcinoma of the prostate. Int J Radiat Oncol Biol Phys, 2001. 50(5): p. 1243-52.

71. Bolla, M., et al., Long-term results with immediate androgen suppression and external irradiation in patients with locally advanced prostate cancer (an EORTC study): a phase III
randomised trial. Lancet, 2002. 360(9327): p. 103-6.

72. Galalae, R.M., et al., Long-term outcome after elective irradiation of the pelvic lymphatics and local dose escalation
using high-dose-rate brachytherapy for locally advanced
prostate cancer. Int J Radiat Oncol Biol Phys, 2002. 52(1):
p. 81-90.

73. Dattoli, M., et al., Long-term outcomes after treatment
with external beam radiation therapy and palladium 103 for
patients with higher risk prostate carcinoma: influence of prostatic acid phosphatase. Cancer, 2003. 97(4): p. 979-83.

74. Hanks, G.E., et al., Phase III trial of long-term adjuvant
androgen deprivation after neoadjuvant hormonal cytoreduc-
tion and radiotherapy in locally advanced carcinoma of the
prostate: the Radiation Therapy Oncology Group Protocol
92-02. J Clin Oncol, 2003. 21(21): p. 3972-8.

75. Valicenti, R.K., et al., RTOG 94-06: is the addition of
neoadjuvant hormonal therapy to dose-escalated 3D conformal radiation therapy for prostate cancer associated with treatment toxicity? Int J Radiat Oncol Biol Phys, 2003. 57(3):
p. 614-20.

76. Critz, F.A. and K. Levinson, 10-year disease-free survival
rates after simultaneous irradiation for prostate cancer with a
focus on calculation methodology. J Urol, 2004. 172(6 Pt 1):
p. 2232-8.

Chapter 8

77. Harris, K.A., V. Weinberg, R.A. Bok, M. Kakefuda, and
E.J. Small, Low dose ketoconazole with replacement doses of
hydrocortisone in patients with progressive androgen independent prostate cancer. J Urol, 2002. 168(2): p. 542-5.

78. Blum, R.A., et al., Increased gastric pH and the bioavailability of fluconazole and ketoconazole. Ann Intern Med, 1991. 114(9): p. 755-7.

79. Lelawongs, P., et al., Effect of food and gastric acidity on absorption of orally administered ketoconazole. Clin Pharm, 1988. 7(3): p. 228-35.

80. Boxenbaum, H., Cytochrome P450 3A4 in vivo ketoconazole competitive inhibition: determination of Ki and dangers associated with high clearance drugs in general. J Pharm Pharm Sci, 1999. 2(2): p. 47-52.

81. Talcott, J.A., et al., Patient-reported impotence and incontinence after nerve-sparing radical prostatectomy. J Natl Cancer Inst, 1997. 89(15): p. 1117-23.

82. Talcott, J.A., et al., Patient-reported symptoms after primary therapy for early prostate cancer: results of a prospective cohort study. J Clin Oncol, 1998. 16(1): p. 275-83.

83. Talcott, J.A., et al., Time course and predictors of symptoms after primary prostate cancer therapy. J Clin Oncol, 2003. 21(21): p. 3979-86.

84. Menon, M. and A.K. Hemal, Vattikuti Institute prostatectomy: a technique of robotic radical prostatectomy: experience in more than 1000 cases. J Endourol, 2004. 18(7): p. 611-9; discussion 619.

85. Menon, M., et al., Vattikuti Institute prostatectomy, a technique of robotic radical prostatectomy for management of localized carcinoma of the prostate: experience of over 1100 cases. Urol Clin North Am, 2004. 31(4): p. 701-17.

86. Tewari, A., S. Kaul, and M. Menon, Robotic radical prostatectomy: a minimally invasive therapy for prostate cancer. Curr Urol Rep, 2005. 6(1): p. 45-8.

Chapter 10

87. Barbeau, P., et al., "Influence of physical training on plasma leptin in obese youths" Can J Appl Physiol 28(3): 382-96.

88. Bullo, M., et al., "Systemic inflammation, adipose tissue tumor necrosis factor, and leptin expression" Obes Res 11(4): 525-31, 2003.

89. Kaaks, R., et al., "Interrelationships between plasma testosterone, SHBG, IGF-I, insulin and leptin in prostate cancer cases and controls" Eur J Cancer Prev 12(4): p. 309-15, 2003.

90. Koutsari, C., et al., "Plasma leptin is influenced by diet composition and exercise" Int J Obes Relat Metab Disord 27(8): 901-6, 2003.

91. Kraemer, R.R., et al., "Effects of high-intensity exercise on leptin and testosterone concentrations in well-trained males" Endocrine 21(3): 261-, 2003.

92. La Cava, A., C. Alviggi, and G. Matarese, "Unraveling the multiple roles of leptin in inflammation and autoimmunity" J Mol Med, 2003.

93. Onuma, M., et al., "Prostate cancer cell-adipocyte interaction: Leptin mediates androgen-independent prostate cancer cell proliferation through c-Jun NH2-terminal kinase" J Biol Chem, 2003.

94. C. Byrne, et al., "Maximal-intensity isometric and dynamic exercise performance after eccentric muscle actions" J Sports Sci 20: 951-9, 2002.

95. G.E. Campos, et al., "Muscular adaptations in response to three different resistance-training regimens: specificity of repetition maximum training zones" Eur J Appl Physiol 88: 50-60, 2002.

96. T.J. Carroll, et al., "Resistance training frequency: strength and myosin heavy chain responses to two and three bouts per week" Eur J Appl Physiol Occup Physiol 78: 270-5, 1998.

97. A. Caterisano, et al., "The effect of back squat depth on the EMG activity of 4 superficial hip and thigh muscles" J Strength Cond Res 16: 428-32, 2002.

98. R.F. Escamilla, "Knee biomechanics of the dynamic squat exercise" Med Sci Sports Exerc 33: 127-41, 2001.

99. I.G. Fatouros, et al., "The effects of strength training, cardiovascular training and their combination on flexibility of inactive older adults" Int J Sports Med 23: 112-9, 2002.

100. S. Flanagan, et al., "Squatting Exercises in Older Adults: Kinematic and Kinetic Comparisons" Med Sci Sports Exerc 35: 635-643, 2003.

101. F.C. Hagerman, et al., "Effects of high-intensity resistance training on untrained older men. I. Strength, cardiovascular, and metabolic responses" J Gerontol A Biol Sci Med Sci 55: B336-46, 2000.

102. K. Hakkinen, et al., "Acute hormone responses to heavy resistance lower and upper extremity exercise in young versus old men" Eur J Appl Physiol Occup Physiol 77: 312-9, 1998.

103. K. Hakkinen, et al., "Effects of heavy resistance/power training on maximal strength, muscle morphology, and hormonal response patterns in 60-75-year-old men and women" Can J Appl Physiol 27: 213-31, 2002.

104. M. Izquierdo, et al., "Effects of strength training on submaximal and maximal endurance performance capacity in middle-aged and older men" J Strength Cond Res 17: 129-39, 2003.

105. N. McCartney, et al., "A longitudinal trial of weight training in the elderly: continued improvements in year 2" J Gerontol A Biol Sci Med Sci 51: B425-33, 1996.

106. A.E. Pels, 3rd, et al., "Effects of leg press training on cycling, leg press, and running peak cardiorespiratory measures" Med Sci Sports Exerc 19: 66-70, 1987.

107. D.A. Wallace, et al., "Patellofemoral joint kinetics while squatting with and without an external load" J Orthop Sports Phys Ther 32: 141-8, 2002.

108. D.S. Willoughby, et al., "Effects of oral creatine and resistance training on myogenic regulatory factor expression" Med Sci Sports Exerc 35: 923-9, 2003.

109. J.L. Vierck, et al., "The effects of ergogenic compounds on myogenic satellite cells" Med Sci Sports Exerc 35: 769-76, 2003.

110. R.J. Snow, et al., "Factors influencing creatine loading into human skeletal muscle" Exerc Sport Sci Rev 31: 154-8, 2003.

111. S.S. Roy, et al., "Protective effect of creatine against inhibition by methylglyoxal of mitochondrial respiration of cardiac cells" Biochem J 372: 661-9, 2003.

112. K.B. Rooney, et al., "Creatine supplementation affects glucose homeostasis but not insulin secretion in humans" Ann Nutr Metab 47: 11-5, 2003.

113. D. Preen, et al., "Creatine supplementation: a comparison of loading and maintenance protocols on creatine uptake by human skeletal muscle" Int J Sport Nutr Exerc Metab 13: 97-111, 2003.

114. A.M. Persky, et al., "Single- and multiple-dose pharmacokinetics of oral creatine" J Clin Pharmacol 43: 29-37, 2003.

115. J.E. Newman, et al., "Effect of creatine ingestion on glucose tolerance and insulin sensitivity in men" Med Sci Sports Exerc 35: 69-74, 2003.

116. W. Derave, et al., "Combined creatine and protein supplementation in conjunction with resistance training promotes muscle GLUT-4 content and glucose tolerance in humans" J Appl Physiol 94: 1910-6, 2003.

1117. M. Wyss, et al., "Health implications of creatine: can oral creatine supplementation protect against neurological and atherosclerotic disease?" Neuroscience 112: 243-60, 2002.

118. B. Walzel, et al., "Novel mitochondrial creatine transport activity. Implications for intracellular creatine compartments and bioenergetics" J Biol Chem 277: 37503-11, 2002.

119. A.C. Passaquin, et al., "Creatine supplementation reduces skeletal muscle degeneration and enhances mitochondrial function in mdx mice" Neuromuscul Disord 12: 174-82, 2002.

120. J.L. Mesa, et al., "Oral creatine supplementation and skeletal muscle metabolism in physical exercise" Sports Med 32: 903-44, 2002.

121. J.M. Lukaszuk, et al., "Effect of creatine supplementation and a lacto-ovo-vegetarian diet on muscle creatine concentration" Int J Sport Nutr Exerc Metab 12: 336-48, 2002.

123. A.M. Jones, et al., "Effect of creatine supplementation on oxygen uptake kinetics during submaximal cycle exercise" J Appl Physiol 92: 2571-7, 2002.

124. D.S. Willoughby, et al., "Effects of oral creatine and resistance training on myosin heavy chain expression" Med Sci Sports Exerc 33: 1674-81, 2001.

125. P. Hespel, et al., "Oral creatine supplementation facilitates the rehabilitation of disuse atrophy and alters the expression of muscle myogenic factors in humans" J Physiol 536: 625-33, 2001.

126. M. Echegaray, et al., "Role of creatine kinase isoenzymes on muscular and cardiorespiratory endurance: genetic and molecular evidence" Sports Med 31: 919-34, 2001.

127. G.R. Steenge, et al., "Protein- and carbohydrate-induced augmentation of whole body creatine retention in humans" J Appl Physiol 89: 1165-71, 2000.

128. M.D. Becque, et al., "Effects of oral creatine supplementation on muscular strength and body composition" Med Sci Sports Exerc 32: 654-8, 2000.

129. C. Rae, et al., "Oral creatine monohydrate supplementation improves brain performance: a double-blind, placebo-controlled, cross-over trial" Proc R Soc Lond B Biol Sci 270:2147-50, 2003.

130. Cardiac disorders and sibutramine. Prescrire Int, 2002. 11(60): p. 117.

131. Appolinario, J.C., et al., A randomized, double-blind, placebo-controlled study of sibutramine in the treatment of binge-eating disorder. Arch Gen Psychiatry, 2003. 60(11): p. 1109-16.

132. Arfken, C.L., C.R. Schuster, and C.E. Johanson, Postmarketing surveillance of abuse liability of sibutramine. Drug Alcohol Depend, 2003. 69(2): p. 169-73.

134. Barkeling, B., et al., Short-term effects of sibutramine (Reductil) on appetite and eating behaviour and the long-term therapeutic outcome. Int J Obes Relat Metab Disord, 2003. 27(6): p. 693-700.

135. Berkowitz, R.I., et al., Behavior therapy and sibutramine for the treatment of adolescent obesity: a randomized controlled trial. Jama, 2003. 289(14): p. 1805-12.

136. Ersoz, H.O., et al., Effect of low-dose metoprolol in combination with sibutramine therapy in normotensive obese patients: a randomized controlled study. Int J Obes Relat Metab Disord, 2004. 28(3): p. 378-83.

137. Finer, N., Sibutramine: its mode of action and efficacy. Int J Obes Relat Metab Disord, 2002. 26 Suppl 4: p. S29-33.

138. Guven, A., et al., Effects of the sibutramine therapy on pulmonary artery pressure in obese patients. Diabetes Obes Metab, 2004. 6(1): p. 50-5.

139. Kaukua, J.K., T.A. Pekkarinen, and A.M. Rissanen, Health-related quality of life in a randomised placebo-controlled trial of sibutramine in obese patients with type II diabetes. Int J Obes Relat Metab Disord, 2004.

140. Kim, S.H., et al., Effect of sibutramine on weight loss and blood pressure: a meta-analysis of controlled trials. Obes Res, 2003. 11(9): p. 1116-23.

141. Narkiewicz, K., Sibutramine and its cardiovascular profile. Int J Obes Relat Metab Disord, 2002. 26 Suppl 4: p. S38-41.

142. Padwal, R., S.K. Li, and D.C. Lau, Long-term pharmacotherapy for overweight and obesity: a systematic review and meta-analysis of randomized controlled trials. Int J Obes Relat Metab Disord, 2003. 27(12): p. 1437-46.

143. Redmon, J.B., et al., One-year outcome of a combination of weight loss therapies for subjects with type 2 diabetes: a randomized trial. Diabetes Care, 2003. 26(9): p. 2505-11.

145. Sabuncu, T., et al., The effects of sibutramine and orlistat on the ultrasonographic findings, insulin resistance and liver enzyme levels in obese patients with non-alcoholic steatohepatitis. Rom J Gastroenterol, 2003. 12(3): p. 189-92.

146. Tambascia, M.A., et al., Sibutramine enhances insulin sensitivity ameliorating metabolic parameters in a double-blind, randomized, placebo-controlled trial. Diabetes Obes Metab, 2003. 5(5): p. 338-44.

147. Warren, E., A. Brennan, and R. Akehurst, Cost-effectiveness of sibutramine in the treatment of obesity. Med Decis Making, 2004. 24(1): p. 9-19.

148. Zannad, F., et al., Effects of sibutramine on ventricular dimensions and heart valves in obese patients during weight reduction. Am Heart J, 2002. 144(3): p. 508-15.

149. Torgerson, J.S., et al., XENical in the prevention of diabetes in obese subjects (XENDOS) study: a randomized study of orlistat as an adjunct to lifestyle changes for the prevention of type 2 diabetes in obese patients. Diabetes Care, 2004. 27(1): p. 155-61.

150. Tiikkainen, M., et al., Effects of equal weight loss with orlistat and placebo on body fat and serum fatty acid composition and insulin resistance in obese women. Am J Clin Nutr, 2004. 79(1): p. 22-30.

151. O'Meara, S., et al., A systematic review of the clinical effectiveness of orlistat used for the management of obesity. Obes Rev, 2004. 5(1): p. 51-68.

152. Mathus-Vliegen, E.M., M.L. Van Ierland-Van Leeuwen, and A. Terpstra, Lipase inhibition by orlistat: effects on gallbladder kinetics and cholecystokinin release in obesity. Aliment Pharmacol Ther, 2004. 19(5): p. 601-11.

153. Kelley, D.E., et al., Effects of moderate weight loss and orlistat on insulin resistance, regional adiposity, and fatty acids in type 2 diabetes. Diabetes Care, 2004. 27(1): p. 33-40.

154. Colak, R. and O. Ozcelik, Effects of short-period exercise training and orlistat therapy on body composition and maximal power production capacity in obese patients. Physiol Res, 2004. 53(1): p. 53-60.

155. Zhi, J., et al., Effects of orlistat, a lipase inhibitor, on the pharmacokinetics of three highly lipophilic drugs (amiodarone, fluoxetine, and simvastatin) in healthy volunteers. J Clin Pharmacol, 2003. 43(4): p. 428-35.

156. Ullrich, A., et al., Impact of carbohydrate and fat intake on weight-reducing efficacy of orlistat. Aliment Pharmacol Ther, 2003. 17(8): p. 1007-13.

157. Maetzel, A., et al., Economic evaluation of orlistat in overweight and obese patients with type 2 diabetes mellitus. Pharmacoeconomics, 2003. 21(7): p. 501-12.

158. Krempf, M., et al., Weight reduction and long-term maintenance after 18 months treatment with orlistat for obesity. Int J Obes Relat Metab Disord, 2003. 27(5): p. 591-7.

159. Goedecke, J.H., et al., Effects of a lipase inhibitor (Orlistat) on cholecystokinin and appetite in response to a high-fat meal. Int J Obes Relat Metab Disord, 2003. 27(12): p. 1479-85.

160. Derosa, G., et al., Randomized, double-blind, placebo-controlled comparison of the action of orlistat, fluvastatin, or both an anthropometric measurements, blood pressure, and lipid profile in obese patients with hypercholesterolemia prescribed a standardized diet. Clin Ther, 2003. 25(4): p. 1107-22.
161. Bloch, K.V., et al., Orlistat in hypertensive overweight/obese patients: results of a randomized clinical trial. J Hypertens, 2003. 21(11): p. 2159-2165.

162. McDuffie, J.R., et al., Effects of orlistat on fat-soluble vitamins in obese adolescents. Pharmacotherapy, 2002. 22(7): p. 814-22.

163. Zhi, J., et al., The effect of orlistat, an inhibitor of dietary fat absorption, on the pharmacokinetics of beta-carotene in healthy volunteers. J Clin Pharmacol, 1996. 36(2): p. 152-9.

164. Miller, E.R., et al., Meta-Analysis: High-Dosage Vitamin E Supplementation May Increase All-Cause Mortality. Annals Internal Medicine To be published January 2005.

165. Takahashi, O., H. Ichikawa, and M. Sasaki, Hemorrhagic toxicity of d-alpha-tocopherol in the rat. Toxicology, 1990. 63(2): p. 157-65.

166. Dowd, P. and Z.B. Zheng, On the mechanism of the anticlotting action of vitamin E quinone. Proc Natl Acad Sci U S A, 1995. 92(18): p. 8171-5.

167. Steiner, M., M. Glantz, and A. Lekos, Vitamin E plus aspirin compared with aspirin alone in patients with transient ischemic attacks. Am J Clin Nutr, 1995. 62(6 Suppl): p. 1381S-1384S.

168. Takahashi, O., Haemorrhagic toxicity of a large dose of alpha-, beta-, gamma- and delta-tocopherols, ubiquinone, beta-carotene, retinol acetate and L-ascorbic acid in the rat. Food Chem Toxicol, 1995. 33(2): p. 121-8.

169. Liede, K.E., et al., Increased tendency towards gingival bleeding caused by joint effect of alpha-tocopherol supplementation and acetylsalicylic acid. Ann Med, 1998. 30(6): p. 542-6.

170. Leppala, J.M., et al., Controlled trial of alpha-tocopherol and beta-carotene supplements on stroke incidence and mortality in male smokers. Arterioscler Thromb Vasc Biol, 2000. 20(1): p. 230-5.

171. Leppala, J.M., et al., Vitamin E and beta carotene supplementation in high risk for stroke: a subgroup analysis of the Alpha-Tocopherol, Beta-Carotene Cancer Prevention Study. Arch Neurol, 2000. 57(10): p. 1503-9.

172. Booth, S.L., et al., Effect of vitamin E supplementation on vitamin K status in adults with normal coagulation status. Am J Clin Nutr, 2004. 80(1): p. 143-8.

173. Tornwall, M.E., et al., Postintervention effect of alpha tocopherol and beta carotene on different strokes: a 6-year follow-up of the Alpha Tocopherol, Beta Carotene Cancer Prevention Study. Stroke, 2004. 35(8): p. 1908-13.

174. Galli, F., et al., The effect of alpha- and gamma-tocopherol and their carboxyethyl hydroxychroman metabolites on prostate cancer cell proliferation. Arch Biochem Biophys, 2004. 423(1): p. 97-102.

175 Giovannucci, E., Gamma-tocopherol: a new player in prostate cancer prevention? J Natl Cancer Inst, 2000. 92(24): p. 1966-7.

176. Gunawardena, K., D.K. Murray, and A.W. Meikle, Vitamin E and other antioxidants inhibit human prostate cancer cells through apoptosis. Prostate, 2000. 44(4): p. 287-95.

177. Gysin, R., A. Azzi, and T. Visarius, Gamma-tocopherol inhibits human cancer cell cycle progression and cell proliferation by down-regulation of cyclins. Faseb J, 2002. 16(14): p. 1952-4.

178. Heinonen, O.P., et al., Prostate cancer and supplementation with alpha-tocopherol and beta-carotene: incidence and mortality in a controlled trial. J Natl Cancer Inst, 1998. 90(6): p. 440-6.

179. Jiang, Q., et al., Gamma-tocopherol, the major form of vitamin E in the US diet, deserves more attention. Am J Clin Nutr, 2001. 74(6): p. 714-22.

180. Ripple, M.O., et al., Androgen-induced oxidative stress in human LNCaP prostate cancer cells is associated with multiple mitochondrial modifications. Antioxid Redox Signal, 1999. 1(1): p. 71-81.

181. Virtamo, J., et al., Incidence of cancer and mortality following alpha-tocopherol and beta-carotene supplementation: a postintervention follow-up. Jama, 2003. 290(4): p. 476-85.

182. Zu, K. and C. Ip, Synergy between selenium and vitamin E in apoptosis induction is associated with activation of distinctive initiator caspases in human prostate cancer cells. Cancer Res, 2003. 63(20): p. 6988-95.

183. Li, H., et al., Manganese superoxide dismutase polymorphism, prediagnostic antioxidant status, and risk of clinical significant prostate cancer. Cancer Res, 2005. 65(6): p. 2498-504. 2. Taufer, M., et al., Is the Val16Ala manganese superoxide dismutase polymorphism associated with the aging process? J Gerontol A Biol Sci Med Sci, 2005. 60(4): p. 432-8.

184 Astorg, P., Dietary n - 6 and n - 3 Polyunsaturated Fatty Acids and Prostate Cancer Risk: A Review of Epidemiological and Experimental Evidence. Cancer Causes Control, 2004. 15(4): p. 367-386.

185. Augustsson, K., et al., A prospective study of intake of fish and marine fatty acids and prostate cancer. Cancer Epidemiol Biomarkers Prev, 2003. 12(1): p. 64-7.

186. Conquer, J.A. and B.J. Holub, Supplementation with an algae source of docosahexaenoic acid increases (n-3) fatty acid status and alters selected risk factors for heart disease in vegetarian subjects. J Nutr, 1996. 126(12): p. 3032-9.

187. Davis, B.C. and P.M. Kris-Etherton, Achieving optimal essential fatty acid status in vegetarians: current knowledge and practical implications. Am J Clin Nutr, 2003. 78(3 Suppl): p. 640S-646S.

188. Fokkema, M.R., et al., Polyunsaturated fatty acid status of Dutch vegans and omnivores. Prostaglandins Leukot Essent Fatty Acids, 2000. 63(5): p. 279-85.

189. Norrish, A.E., et al., Prostate cancer risk and consumption of fish oils: a dietary biomarker-based case-control study. Br J Cancer, 1999. 81(7): p. 1238-42.

190. Sonoda, T., et al., A case-control study of diet and prostate cancer in Japan: possible protective effect of traditional Japanese diet. Cancer Sci, 2004. 95(3): p. 238-42.

191. Terry, P., et al., Fatty fish consumption and risk of prostate cancer. Lancet, 2001. 357(9270): p. 1764-6.

192. Adams, K.F., et al., Soy isoflavones do not modulate prostate-specific antigen concentrations in older men in a randomized controlled trial. Cancer Epidemiol Biomarkers Prev, 2004. 13(4): p. 644-8.

193. Hussain, M., et al., Soy isoflavones in the treatment of prostate cancer. Nutr Cancer, 2003. 47(2): p. 111-7.

194. Hermansen, K., et al., Effects of soy and other natural products on LDL:HDL ratio and other lipid parameters: a literature review. Adv Ther, 2003. 20(1): p. 50-78.

195. Azadbakht, L., et al., Beneficiary effect of dietary soy protein on lowering plasma levels of lipid and improving kidney function in type II diabetes with nephropathy. Eur J Clin Nutr, 2003. 57(10): p. 1292-4.

196. Yamada, T., et al., Prevalence of dementia in the older Japanese-Brazilian population. Psychiatry Clin Neurosci, 2002. 56(1): p. 71-5.

197. White, L.R., et al., Brain aging and midlife tofu consumption. J Am Coll Nutr, 2000. 19(2): p. 242-55.

199. Messina, M. and V. Messina, Soyfoods, soybean isoflavones, and bone health: a brief overview. J Ren Nutr, 2000. 10(2): p. 63-8.

200. Kim, H., et al., Attenuation of neurodegeneration-relevant modifications of brain proteins by dietary soy. Biofactors, 2000. 12(1-4): p. 243-50.

201. Wong, W.W., et al., Cholesterol-lowering effect of soy protein in normocholesterolemic and hypercholesterolemic men. Am J Clin Nutr, 1998. 68(6 Suppl): p. 1385S-1389S.

202. Dragan, I., et al., Studies regarding the efficiency of Supro isolated soy protein in Olympic athletes. Rev Roum Physiol, 1992. 29(3-4): p. 63-70.

203. Asencio, C., et al., Silencing of ubiquinone biosynthesis genes extends life span in Caenorhabditis elegans. Faseb J, 2003. 17(9): p. 1135-7.

204. Driver, C. and A. Georgiou, How to re-energise old mitochondria without shooting yourself in the foot. Biogerontology, 2002. 3(1-2): p. 103-6.

205. Ebadi, M., et al., Ubiquinone (coenzyme q10) and mito-chondria in oxidative stress of parkinson's disease. Biol Signals Recept, 2001. 10(3-4): p. 224-53.

206. Hodgson, J.M., et al., Coenzyme Q10 improves blood pressure and glycaemic control: a controlled trial in subjects with type 2 diabetes. Eur J Clin Nutr, 2002. 56(11): p. 1137-42.

207. Krum, H. and J.J. McMurray, Statins and chronic heart failure: do we need a large-scale outcome trial? J Am Coll Cardiol, 2002. 39(10): p. 1567-73.

208. Langsjoen, P.H. and A.M. Langsjoen, The clinical use of HMG CoA-reductase inhibitors and the associated depletion of coenzyme Q10. A review of animal and human publica-tions. Biofactors, 2003. 18(1-4): p. 101-11.

209. Larsen, P.L. and C.F. Clarke, Extension of life-span in Caenorhabditis elegans by a diet lacking coenzyme Q. Science, 2002. 295(5552): p. 120-3.

210. Liu, X., et al., Evolutionary conservation of the clk-1-dependent mechanism of longevity: loss of mclk1 increases cellular fitness and lifespan in mice. Genes Dev, 2005.
9. Miles, M.V., et al., Coenzyme Q10 changes are associated with metabolic syndrome. Clin Chim Acta, 2004. 344(1-2): p. 173-9.

211. Nakai, D., et al., coq7/clk-1 regulates mitochondrial respi-ration and the generation of reactive oxygen species via coen-zyme Q. Aging Cell, 2004. 3(5): p. 273-81.

212. Nakai, D., et al., Mouse homologue of coq7/clk-1, longevity gene in Caenorhabditis elegans, is essential for coenzyme Q synthesis, maintenance of mitochondrial integrity, and neurogenesis. Biochem Biophys Res Commun, 2001. 289(2): p. 463-71.

213. Rosenfeldt, F., et al., Systematic review of effect of coenzyme Q10 in physical exercise, hypertension and heart failure. Biofactors, 2003. 18(1-4): p. 91-100.

214. Ruiz-Pesini, E., et al., Effects of purifying and adaptive selection on regional variation in human mtDNA. Science, 2004. 303(5655): p. 223-6.

215. Rundek, T., et al., Atorvastatin decreases the coenzyme Q10 level in the blood of patients at risk for cardiovascular disease and stroke. Arch Neurol, 2004. 61(6): p. 889-92.

216. Silver, M.A., et al., Effect of atorvastatin on left ventricular diastolic function and ability of coenzyme Q10 to reverse that dysfunction. Am J Cardiol, 2004. 94(10): p. 1306-10.

217. Campbell, R.J. and K.B. Sneed, Acute congestive heart failure induced by rofecoxib. J Am Board Fam Pract, 2004. 17(2): p. 131-5.

218. Clark, D.W., D. Layton, and S.A. Shakir, Do some inhibitors of COX-2 increase the risk of thromboembolic events? Linking pharmacology with pharmacoepidemiology. Drug Saf, 2004. 27(7): p. 427-56.

219. Dorai, T., N. Gehani, and A. Katz, Therapeutic potential of curcumin in human prostate cancer-I. curcumin induces apoptosis in both androgen-dependent and androgen-independent prostate cancer cells. Prostate Cancer Prostatic Dis, 2000. 3(2): p. 84-93.

220. Fitzgerald, G.A., Coxibs and cardiovascular disease. N Engl J Med, 2004. 351(17): p. 1709-11.

221. Graham, D.J., et al., Risk of acute myocardial infarction and sudden cardiac death in patients treated with cyclo-oxygenase 2 selective and non-selective non-steroidal anti-inflammatory drugs: nested case-control study. Lancet, 2005. 365(9458): p. 475-81.

222. Hour, T.C., et al., Curcumin enhances cytotoxicity of chemotherapeutic agents in prostate cancer cells by inducing p21(WAF1/CIP1) and C/EBPbeta expressions and suppressing NF-kappaB activation. Prostate, 2002. 51(3): p. 211-8.

223. Mukherjee, D., S.E. Nissen, and E.J. Topol, Risk of cardiovascular events associated with selective COX-2 inhibitors. Jama, 2001. 286(8): p. 954-9.

224. Mukhopadhyay, A., et al., Curcumin downregulates cell survival mechanisms in human prostate cancer cell lines. Oncogene, 2001. 20(52): p. 7597-609.

225. Nakamura, K., et al., Curcumin down-regulates AR gene expression and activation in prostate cancer cell lines. Int J Oncol, 2002. 21(4): p. 825-30.

226. Ramsewak, R.S., D.L. DeWitt, and M.G. Nair, Cytotoxicity, antioxidant and anti-inflammatory activities of curcumins I-III from Curcuma longa. Phytomedicine, 2000. 7(4): p. 303-8.

227. Roumie, C.L., et al., Prescriptions for Chronic High-Dose Cyclooxygenase-2 Inhibitors are Often Inappropriate and Potentially Dangerous. J Gen Intern Med, 2005. 20(10): p. 879-83.

228. Shoba, G., et al., Influence of piperine on the pharmacokinetics of curcumin in animals and human volunteers. Planta Med, 1998. 64(4): p. 353-6.

229. Solomon, D.H., et al., Relationship between COX-2 specific inhibitors and hypertension. Hypertension, 2004. 44(2): p. 140-5.

230. Wolfe, F., S. Zhao, and D. Pettitt, Blood pressure destabilization and edema among 8538 users of celecoxib, rofecoxib, and nonselective nonsteroidal antiinflammatory drugs (NSAID) and nonusers of NSAID receiving ordinary clinical care. J Rheumatol, 2004. 31(6): p. 1143-51.

231 Zhou, S., L.Y. Lim, and B. Chowbay, Herbal modulation of P-glycoprotein. Drug Metab Rev, 2004. 36(1): p. 57-104.

232. Aggarwal, B.B., et al., Role of resveratrol in prevention and therapy of cancer: preclinical and clinical studies. Anticancer Res, 2004. 24(5A): p. 2783-840.

233. Borra, M.T., B.C. Smith, and J.M. Denu, Mechanism of human SIRT1 activation by resveratrol. J Biol Chem, 2005. 280(17): p. 17187-95.

234. Bradamante, S., L. Barenghi, and A. Villa, Cardiovascular protective effects of resveratrol. Cardiovasc Drug Rev, 2004. 22(3): p. 169-88.

235. Burns, J., et al., Plant foods and herbal sources of resveratrol. J Agric Food Chem, 2002. 50(11): p. 3337-40.

236. Coimbra, S.R., et al., The action of red wine and purple grape juice on vascular reactivity is independent of plasma lipids in hypercholesterolemic patients. Braz J Med Biol Res, 2005. 38(9): p. 1339-47.

237. Gao, S., G.Z. Liu, and Z. Wang, Modulation of androgen receptor-dependent transcription by resveratrol and genistein in prostate cancer cells. Prostate, 2004. 59(2): p. 214-25.

238. Hansen, A.S., et al., Effect of red wine and red grape extract on blood lipids, haemostatic factors, and other risk factors for cardiovascular disease. Eur J Clin Nutr, 2005. 59(3): p. 449-55.

239. Howitz, K.T., et al., Small molecule activators of sirtuins extend Saccharomyces cerevisiae lifespan. Nature, 2003. 425(6954): p. 191-6.

240. Jones, S.B., et al., Resveratrol-induced gene expression profiles in human prostate cancer cells. Cancer Epidemiol Biomarkers Prev, 2005. 14(3): p. 596-604.

241. Kaeberlein, M., et al., Substrate-specific activation of sirtuins by resveratrol. J Biol Chem, 2005. 280(17): p. 17038-45.

242. Kim, Y.A., et al., Antiproliferative effect of resveratrol in human prostate carcinoma cells. J Med Food, 2003. 6(4): p. 273-80.

243. Meng, X., et al., Urinary and plasma levels of resveratrol and quercetin in humans, mice, and rats after ingestion of pure compounds and grape juice. J Agric Food Chem, 2004. 52(4): p. 935-42.

245. Schoonen, W.M., et al., Alcohol consumption and risk of prostate cancer in middle-aged men. Int J Cancer, 2005. 113(1): p. 133-40.

246. Stewart, J.R., M.C. Artime, and C.A. O'Brian, Resveratrol: a candidate nutritional substance for prostate cancer prevention. J Nutr, 2003. 133(7 Suppl): p. 2440S-2443S.

247. Vitaglione, P., et al., Bioavailability of trans-resveratrol from red wine in humans. Mol Nutr Food Res, 2005. 49(5): p. 495-504.

248. Walle, T., et al., High absorption but very low bioavailability of oral resveratrol in humans. Drug Metab Dispos, 2004. 32(12): p. 1377-82.

249. Wenzel, E., et al., Bioactivity and metabolism of trans-resveratrol orally administered to Wistar rats. Mol Nutr Food Res, 2005. 49(5): p. 482-94.

250. Wenzel, E. and V. Somoza, Metabolism and bioavailability of trans-resveratrol. Mol Nutr Food Res, 2005. 49(5): p. 472-81.

251. Wood, J.G., et al., Sirtuin activators mimic caloric restriction and delay ageing in metazoans. Nature, 2004. 430(7000): p. 686-9.

252. Bhatia, N., et al., Inhibition of human carcinoma cell growth and DNA synthesis by silibinin, an active constituent of milk thistle: comparison with silymarin. Cancer Lett, 1999. 147(1-2): p. 77-84.

253. Maitrejean, M., et al., The flavanolignan silybin and its hemisynthetic derivatives, a novel series of potential modulators of P-glycoprotein. Bioorg Med Chem Lett, 2000. 10(2): p. 157-60.

254. Singh, R.P. and R. Agarwal, A cancer chemopreventive agent silibinin, targets mitogenic and survival signaling in prostate cancer. Mutat Res, 2004. 555(1-2): p. 21-32.

255. Singh, R.P., et al., Dietary feeding of silibinin inhibits advance human prostate carcinoma growth in athymic nude mice and increases plasma insulin-like growth factor-binding protein-3 levels. Cancer Res, 2002. 62(11): p. 3063-9.

256. Sridar, C., et al., Silybin inactivates cytochromes P450 3A4 and 2C9 and inhibits major hepatic glucuronosyltransferases. Drug Metab Dispos, 2004. 32(6): p. 587-94.

257. Venkataramanan, R., et al., Milk thistle, a herbal supplement, decreases the activity of CYP3A4 and uridine diphosphoglucuronosyl transferase in human hepatocyte cultures. Drug Metab Dispos, 2000. 28(11): p. 1270-3.

258. Zhou, S., L.Y. Lim, and B. Chowbay, Herbal modulation of P-glycoprotein. Drug Metab Rev, 2004. 36(1): p. 57-104.

Notes

Printed in the United States
62947LVS00003B/163-240